Praise for **Thoughtload**

"We felt seen reading *Thoughtload*—and then felt so much better. Liane Davey names the real source of modern overwhelm and gives leaders a smart, practical, humane playbook for a saner way to work."

FRANCES FREI and ANNE MORRISS, bestselling authors of *Move Fast & Fix Things* and hosts of the hit podcast *Fixable*

"Liane Davey has once again done what she does best: cracked open the messy truth of how we think, work, and relate, handing us a clear, compassionate path forward. *Thoughtload* is a mirror for every high-achiever who's ever believed that more effort, more ideas, more involvement was the answer... only to find themselves exhausted and resentful. Her insights into the mental clutter we carry, especially in the name of ambition, care, and responsibility, are both validating and galvanizing. This book is sharp, timely and, like Davey herself, deeply wise."

LAURA GASSNER OTTING,
Wall Street Journal*–bestselling author of *Wonderhell

"Overwhelmed? It may not be your workload. It may be your thoughtload. This is a brilliant book, and the perfect rejoinder to all that productivity BS."

MICHAEL BUNGAY STANIER, bestselling author of *The Coaching Habit*

"I've known Liane Davey for years, and I've always admired her ability to name what sits beneath the noise. At a time when leaders are quick to blame burnout on speed, scale, or AI, *Thoughtload* points to a more enduring source of strain: the accumulation of unprocessed thoughts, emotions, and decisions that quietly tax judgment and attention. As technology accelerates and organizations grow more complex, the cost of that invisible load shows up where it matters most... in clarity, decision-making, and leadership presence. Davey doesn't offer shortcuts or optimization hacks. She offers something rarer and more valuable for CEOs: a way to think more clearly under pressure, to lead with steadiness in complexity, and to create the conditions where great work can happen. *Thoughtload* is one of the most important reads for leaders who need to understand that the future of work will be shaped less by better tools, and more by better thinking."

MITCH JOEL, cofounder of ThinkersOne and author of *Six Pixels of Separation* and *Ctrl Alt Delete* thoughtload

thought

Liane Davey

load

MANAGE THE MADNESS AND FREE YOUR TEAM TO DO GREAT WORK

PAGE TWO

Some names and identifying details have been changed to protect the privacy of individuals.

Cataloguing in publication information is available from Library and Archives Canada.
ISBN 978-1-77458-651-8 (paperback)
ISBN 978-1-77458-758-4 (ebook)

Page Two
pagetwo.com

Cover design by Taysia Louie
Interior design by Peter Cocking
Printed and bound in Canada by Friesens
Distributed in Canada by Raincoast Books
Distributed in the US and internationally by Macmillan

26 27 28 29 30 5 4 3 2 1

thoughtload.com

For my mom, who has always lowered my thoughtload at the expense of raising her own.

Contents

thoughtload

The Real Reason We're Overwhelmed

Twelve leaders of a publicly traded tech company are assembled in a harshly lit basement boardroom. The ceiling is low, the mood lower. The company recently went public, but the high of a momentary unicorn valuation has faded. Growth has slowed. The pressure is mounting. I'm here to help them reset their strategy.

During the check-in, Bob, the CTO, relates the situation to a scenario he's trained for as a private pilot. "We're working super hard," he says, "but we're not getting anywhere. Pilots call that being 'behind the power curve.' You're at full throttle, just barely maintaining altitude. There's no extra power left to climb. If you don't reduce drag, you stall. And if you don't act fast, you crash."

The room falls quiet. Everyone gets it.

Managers everywhere are flying behind the power curve. Full throttle. Nose up. No lift.

Bob says they need to point the nose down, do fewer things, and clean up the drag. As compelling as Bob's comments are, everyone's thinking the same thing. Can we afford to do less? Isn't that risky? Won't we fall behind our competitors?

Then Kurt, the head of marketing, leans forward. He's usually upbeat, an ideas guy. But Bob's candor has set the tone.

He clears his throat and says, "Lately, I wake up already overwhelmed. I spend the day choosing who I'm going to disappoint. There's never enough time or resources. Some days I'm holding everything together, and some days I'm just holding on."

That's the management experience in a nutshell. Lofty targets. Emotional turbulence. And not enough fuel in the tank to get where you're going.

You've tried working harder, being more efficient, and picking up the slack. You've tried to protect your team, shield them from the chaos, and absorb what you can. But you're exhausted, and despite all the effort, your to-do list isn't getting shorter, and productivity is flat or declining. Your effort isn't converting into lift.

While the obvious conclusion might be that workloads are too high and expectations are unreasonable, the data doesn't back that up. Most of us aren't getting more done. Productivity is flat or down in most parts of the economy.

Here's another possibility. What if it's not the workload that's killing you? Most people I talk to would be thrilled if they could just do the work.

What if it's not the workload? What if it's the thoughtload?

What Is Thoughtload?

Thoughtload is a silent tax on your performance and productivity. It is the combined impact of three interrelated factors:

1. **Cognitive demands**: The endless inputs competing for your attention.
2. **Emotional burdens**: The drama you're absorbing, managing, and suppressing.
3. **Energy reserves**: The physical and mental strength to keep going.

$$\textbf{Thoughtload} = \frac{\textbf{Cognitive demands + Emotional burdens}}{\textbf{Energy reserves}}$$

As the equation shows, the higher the cognitive demands and emotional burdens you deal with, and the lower your energy reserves, the higher your thoughtload.

As a manager, you're burdened not just by your own thoughtload but by every team member's thoughtload as well. Everyone you contact is in the same boat: Their attention is divided, their nerves are frayed, and their tanks are empty.

As Bob would say, it's all drag, no lift.

In non-pilot terms, people are distracted, triggered, and burned out.

Managers are the most leveraged role in organizations. And the most overlooked. You're expected to be productive, empathetic, strategic, decisive—and you're often left to figure out how to do all of that on your own.

This book is built to help you

- cut through noise and reclaim your focus,
- process emotional triggers instead of absorbing them, and
- recharge your energy and model healthy boundaries.

Doing this, you can create conditions where your team can *actually* thrive.

To wrangle your thoughtload (and that of others) into submission, you must understand the beast you're battling. Let's explore thoughtload's treacherous triad—distracted attention, triggered emotions, and depleted energy—and consider how each amplifies the negative effects of the others.

Distracted Attention

You're trying, I know. You're trying to get stuff done, but so many things are vying for your attention, so many distractions are diluting your focus. If you're like the average manager of knowledge workers, the reality is sad.

You're spending half your workweek in meetings (22 hours on average), many of which take up what could have been the most productive hours of your day, and few of which add value. Add to that the torrent of emails, Slack or Teams messages (11 hours on average), and 33 hours of your week are already gone. When are you supposed to manage people, do work, or pee?

When you're miraculously liberated from being in a meeting and you have time, you might not be able to get much more done. One study suggests you're interrupted every 11 minutes and are only able to return to your task 25 minutes later. Yup, do the math—even your interruptions get interrupted. And it doesn't take an intrusive coworker or an ill-timed DM to shatter your focus; you might be distracting yourself. The way we work now requires that you toggle between different screens and inputs between 1,200 and 3,000 times each day. Each time, you lose 2 seconds to make the physical switch and significantly more to make the mental switch. Even if you only lose 2 seconds, you're doing nothing but toggling for more than 3 hours a week. Three hours! Imagine what else you could accomplish if you could get even half of it back?

While you're busy attending meetings, fending off interruptions, and somehow still trying to lead your team to glory, your organization is shifting the goalposts. According to research by Gartner, you're likely to face ten enterprise-level transformations each year, with buy-in from only 35 percent of your employees. Ten transformations is a ridiculously ambitious change portfolio, but even more shocking is that this is a fivefold increase from just six years prior, when the average organization had two transformations a year, and managers could count on buy-in from a solid 75 percent of employees.

While your days pull you in a million directions, perhaps the worst of it is when you try to be still at night. How do you shut off the noisy narrator when falling asleep? Maybe you've started listening to the world's most monotone history podcasts to lull you back to sleep (message me to swap suggestions—I've got a long list!) The noisy narrator problem is even worse on Sunday nights, when many people experience the Sunday Scaries at the thought of returning to work on Monday.

Taken together, there are endless attempts to draw on your time and attention, both by those around you as well as by the voice inside your head. I hope you don't experience all of them, or if you do, that you don't get the full brunt of each of them; but you probably have some version of a desperately distracted life, and so do the members of your team.

Lost in the Matrix

What's making this problem so acute? How did it get so bad? You are so distracted for many reasons. Some of them are obvious.

You already know that tiny computer in your hand is designed to make you crave endless stimulation. (The psychologist in me feels compelled to tell you that, contrary to popular wisdom, you don't get a dopamine hit from receiving a notification; you get the dopamine just from thinking there *could be* a notification.) You also know that leaders are throwing more "priorities" at you than you can handle. What does it even mean to have seven priorities at once? (And when did the boss lose sight of the fact that only one thing can come first?)

But there are other highlights (or should I say lowlights?).

We increasingly work in cross-functional teams and matrix structures, so while having seven priorities instead of one at a time is a problem, you have seven from your primary job and seven more from each of the account teams, regional councils, and communities of practice you belong to. You're matrixed, dotted-lined, and voluntold into additional teams, each with its own burden of meetings, emails, and Slack channels calling to you. Unfettered cross-functional collaboration is creating organizational entropy and robbing you of your focus.

And it's not just your colleagues who are distracting you. Remember when "Take Your Kid to Work Day" was one day a year? Before cell phones and hybrid work, we expected family responsibilities to be left at home (except for the odd flooding basement or a call from the kid's vice principal after an "unfortunate incident" with Timmy on the playground).

Now, every day is Take Your Kid to Work Day. You get texts while in meetings: "Where's the peanut butter?" or "Can you drive me to Pete's tonight?" If you don't answer promptly, you get the follow-up, "??" to ensure you're still breathing (because something dire must be happening if you haven't responded to your darling child within 47 seconds). The Surgeon General of the United States has even issued a warning about how our parenting approach is causing high levels of stress.

When did every day become Take Your Kid to Work Day?

Plus, elder care, family responsibilities, and even monitoring the webcam at the doggie daycare can steal our attention throughout the workday.

And as long as your attention is divided, your productivity will be constrained, your anxiety will rise, and your energy will dwindle. Which brings us to another element in the treacherous triad of thoughtload—triggered emotions.

Triggered Emotions

What's going on in our workplaces? Everyone seems so emotional. Things that were once innocuous now stir the pot, cause offense, or even start a row. The tiniest thing sets off an avalanche of emotions. Based on what I see, most managers are dealing with a lot of drama.

Nearly a quarter of people experience anger or sadness at work on a given day, so if you've got a team of four people, odds are you're constantly in the thick of it. One person's foul or fragile mood can spread, leaving you with an entire team of anxious, angered, or demoralized members. An extensive global survey reveals that employees' emotional intelligence in dealing with such dynamics has declined for four consecutive years. Not only is there more snow in the emotional avalanche, but we've got smaller shovels. Well, it's no surprise, then, that almost a third of people have reached the point of emotional exhaustion.

While helping individual team members with their own issues is challenging, you also referee conflicts and hurt feelings between team members (on average, dealing with conflicts eats up 4 hours of a manager's time per week). There's undoubtedly some productive conflict in there, but much of it is probably avoidable interpersonal drama. Although people having overt emotional outbursts might require a lot of your energy, those people might be easier to handle than the employees who suppress their emotional reactions, making it more likely their feelings will erupt in less socially acceptable ways, including through passive-aggressive behavior you can't see but know is under the surface and spreading in the shadows.

The emotional onslaught can also come from outside your team. You need to defend against abusive behaviors from colleagues and leaders who have high targets to hit and little patience left for anything that slows them down. What can be even worse is when the attacks come from customers or clients. Addressing a toxic environment when the problematic people are the ones paying the bills is a particular challenge.

A heartbreaking example of this is in the long-term care industry. Deborah Bakti, author and podcaster, often talks about nurses, personal support workers, and administrators who do incredibly taxing work supporting vulnerable people in their final years. She helps them deal with physical and emotional responses from residents, patients, and family members who are themselves emotionally dysregulated. It's a lot to cope with. Sometimes, the heaviest emotional burden comes from dealing with our customers.

Now, if I'm going to be of any assistance, you and I are going to have to be honest with each other and admit that you, too, are on this emotional rollercoaster. You are susceptible to the same emotionally heavy experiences as your employees. Some surveys indicate that middle managers are at the highest risk of burnout of any group in the workplace. In your exhaustion, you are more likely to be impatient, frustrated, angry, suspicious, sad, or sensitive than usual. And when it gets the better of you, you become even more emotional because you're disappointed in yourself.

I notice this as a parent, wife, and daughter, too. When I am emotionally exhausted and reacting less patiently and graciously than I would like, my family is forgiving. The worst part is how I beat myself up afterward. Feeling upset about getting upset is a torturous loop. But that's where we're at.

Why Are We So Triggered? (AKA "See Above")

We don't have to look far for the first cause of our heightened anxiety: rising cognitive demands, distractions, and disruptions. *See above*. When we try to attend to too many things, our increased arousal reinforces our anxiety. The more we pay attention to, the more we see threats and risks.

We're also living in a world that seems to be angry all the time, whether it's in the 24-hour news cycle, posts on social media, or your uncle Larry at Thanksgiving dinner. We're bombarded with emotionality that's hard to shake.

The more you pay attention to, the more threats you see.

Covid-19 disrupted normal human patterns and not only severed our relationships with offices and hard pants but also with each other. For those who could work from home during the pandemic, the way we worked changed significantly, and it's only slowly finding a new equilibrium. Many of us have colleagues or direct reports whom we've never met in person, so we don't know them or trust them in quite the same way.

With less time together in offices, we have fewer opportunities for downtime to build trust or casual interactions to restore it when it's eroded. We also rely more on digital communication, which is often misinterpreted negatively, triggering emotional reactions, and causing rifts in our relationships.

Contributing to emotionality is also the fear of not staying afloat financially in a time of rising costs and employment insecurity. Nearly 40 percent of people are nervous about how they'll pay the mortgage next month or about how they'll ever be able to afford a house in the first place. Being stressed about basic human needs means that all other stressors are piled on top of an already high baseline.

Workplace Rollercoaster

Before you even walk in the office door, you and your employees have already confronted all of the above emotionally charged issues. But the workplace has a few anxiety-provoking tricks up its sleeve, too.

Based on my experiences, organizations are promoting feedback more than ever before. That seems like a good thing. There are monthly one-on-ones, quarterly development updates, 360° surveys, annual performance reviews, and software that allows anyone to send anonymous feedback at any time. In customer-facing roles, employees must also contend with Net Promoter Scores, feedback cards, and online reviews.

But instead of giving feedback to promote self-awareness, insight, and learning, organizations have unleashed a torrent of judgment. People comment about what they like or don't like or whether the target of their opinions is worthy or unworthy, often using these opportunities to discharge some of their own emotional energy. This barrage of judgment doesn't promote learning; it creates fear and self-doubt.

The matrix structures that dilute attention also contribute to heightened emotions. In a cross-functional team, your employees (and especially you as a manager) are expected to fight for your team to secure resources and win trade-offs if you're going to accomplish your objectives. You must influence without authority and advocate effectively to avoid letting your team down. That conflict is often heated, sometimes personal, and almost always uncomfortable. Confronting it directly is anxiety-provoking, but avoiding it and getting into conflict debt means stewing in resentment.

Either way, greater exposure to (even healthy) conflict at work is increasing everyone's emotional load.

Now that we've talked about the top of the thoughtload equation—attention and emotions—let's talk about the bottom, energy. The relative weight of your thoughtload depends on how much physical, mental, and emotional energy you have to carry the load.

Depleted Energy

In terms of the cognitive demands and the emotional burdens of work and life, we're carrying a heavy weight. But somehow it feels like it used to take less of a toll on our bodies and minds. Many people I talk to are burned out, exhausted, and running on empty. If your world resembles the average manager's, your tank is on empty.

You're often exhausted even at the start of the day. You're fighting to protect 7 hours of sleep, but when you get them, they're interrupted and restless. That means you often don't have the energy to do the things that invigorate you. You skip the gym, push back friend time, and think wistfully of the hobby you've been meaning to get back to—when things calm down (lol). And when you don't exercise, socialize, or otherwise metabolize, you're also making it harder to get to sleep.

It's not just your physical energy that's in the crapper; your motivation may be suffering too. And even if you're still passionate about your work, that fire within doesn't protect you from feeling stressed. Passion isn't enough to prevent exhaustion; it might even make it worse.

When energy is running low, your body tries desperately to conserve it by slowing things down or taking shortcuts.

You're probably seeing the effects in your team's poor planning, impaired judgment, low concentration, and even increased risk-taking. Even more worrisome, burnout isn't just making you all tired; it's making you cynical, detached, and less confident in your abilities.

Maybe you compensate for low physical and mental energy with quick fixes: carbs and caffeine to boost your energy during the day, then a second glass of wine and some scrolling to try to calm yourself down in the evening. These strategies often lead to poor-quality sleep and perpetuate the problem.

Burnout isn't just making you tired; it's making you cynical, detached, and less confident.

The fatigue you're experiencing is physical, mental, and emotional, and makes the cognitive demands and emotional weight of life much harder to bear.

The Dead Work Problem

When you think of the number of people, teams, and organizations with unachievable objectives, it's no surprise we're all burning out. These lofty goals might be associated with delivering quarterly results in publicly traded companies, finding efficiencies in privately held institutions or government, or trying to keep up with surging demands in a charitable organization. The threat of falling short of these objectives keeps you running fast.

The problem is that few organizations understand which expenditures of energy are worthwhile and which aren't. I've worked with many companies that have hired huge consulting firms to restructure their business, fix their "spans and layers," or optimize costs. My experience is that those firms help companies reduce the number of boxes on the organizational chart, but do nothing to help managers identify what work can be eliminated, or help leaders accept that they have fewer people and will need to do less. As a result, good people keep toiling away on ineffective tasks. I might sum it up by saying that leaders think they have a dead wood issue when, in fact, they have a dead work issue. It's not that they have incompetent or lazy people; they have trivial and ineffective tasks.

You Can Get Less Drag, More Lift

Although I hear and empathize with people bemoaning their workload, most people I speak with would be thrilled if they could just do the work. Many are invigorated by challenging, meaningful, and yes, even hard work.

My promise to you is that you can enact strategies to manage your thoughtload and get more important work done: Reduce the drag and get more lift. You can also coach your team members to do the same. This book will show you how.

I'm profoundly aware that reading a book that asks you to change how you are doing things might feel like I'm adding to your thoughtload rather than relieving it. My intent is not to throw you an anvil while you're drowning. So, I've built this book with managing thoughtload in mind.

Here's what you'll see:

Small chunks. Concise chapters so you can stop any time. No long chapters or dense text.

Ideas, then tools. Lots of *what* and *so what* with an online toolkit for the *now what*. You can access that toolkit at thoughtload.com.

No judgment. Stories of my fails (some more epic than others), so you know I'm in this madness with you.

Prescriptive methods. Direct and directive because that's what you need when thoughtload is high.

You first, then your team. Strategies to get your own house in order and then to help your team.

The most urgent and vital thing you can do is to manage your thoughtload and then help your team to do the same.

Ready to dive in? Maybe a quick nap first? Nah, let's go!

If time management
came in pill form,
we'd all be taking it.

PART 1

Focus Your Distracted Attention

While our endgame is for you to reduce your team's thoughtload, you cannot manage the madness if you're caught up in it. Just think of all the ways your thoughtload impacts your team members. If your attention is diluted across a vast range of issues and initiatives, your team won't know what to prioritize. If you're nervous, impatient, demoralized, or hostile, you'll pass that emotionality on to your people. If you're run down, exhausted, and uninspired, how do you expect your direct reports to have pep in their step?

You need to tackle your thoughtload first. But where to start, given that your attention, emotions, and energy are so intimately intertwined? I always tackle attention first, because you have no hope of taming emotions or restoring energy if you don't manage your attention. But if triggered emotions or depleted energy feel like a more acute problem for you at the moment, feel free to skip ahead to those parts and then come back to this one. And, heck, if you really can't wait, skip ahead to parts 4, 5, and 6 to read about tools to manage your team—just make sure you come back here because, like I said, you can't contain the chaos if you're causing it.

Tackle your thoughtload before trying to help your team.

The Achievable Ambition: Focused and Flowing

Before we talk about how to effectively focus your attention, let's agree on what "good focus" would look like. I'm not promising you that you can achieve Zen master status, but I'm promising you that you can create a world where you experience periods of deep concentration, leading to productive work and a sense of accomplishment. What if you could experience this:

- Delivering multiple high-quality pieces of work you're proud of each week
- Feeling the satisfaction of accomplishing something worthwhile
- Creating enough slack to accommodate urgent issues and disruptions to your plans
- Strengthening connections and engaging fully in conversations at work and home

- Falling asleep quickly because the intrusive thoughts have simmered down

That's what I want for you. And that's where we're headed. Let's start with a quick synopsis of the science underpinning the techniques and then get to the nitty-gritty.

Science Synopsis

What's going on in your body and mind when your attention is distracted?

To put it simply, your brain is a mono-tasker, not a multitasker. For the most part, you can pay attention to only one thing at a time. Sure, you can walk and chew gum, but that's because you don't need to pay conscious attention to do either. If you switch out gum chewing for texting, you'll get a different result. Your attention goes to texting, not walking, and you're okay until there's a bump on the sidewalk. I learned this the hard way when I went flying (seriously cartwheel-esque rotation) over a sandwich board in front of my local café. I'd hoped no one noticed, but mortifyingly, the next day, the sandwich board had a message for me: "Be careful out there, don't text and walk." (I promised you I'd share my thoughtload fails, right?)

While you feel like you're multitasking, what you're actually doing is toggling—switching your attention from one thing to the other. It turns out that toggling is inefficient:

- Your productivity decreases.
- It takes longer to complete both tasks.
- The quality of your work suffers as well.

And multitasking doesn't just *slow* you down; it *gets* you down. Attempts to multitask are associated with increased stress, heightened anxiety, and even temporary depressive symptoms.

When it comes to thoughtload, multitasking is part of a vicious cycle. When you're anxious about how much you have to do, you tend to multitask to alleviate anxiety. Ironically, instead of helping you plow through more work, multitasking can make you less productive, leaving you with *more* to do, which in turn makes you even more stressed. Brutal!

Multitasking doesn't just slow you down, it gets you down.

If multitasking doesn't work, why do we keep attempting it? That's another aspect of the vicious cycle. The more tired and overwhelmed you are (the energy component of thoughtload), the poorer your brain is at calibrating what you should attend to and what you should ignore. Instead of focusing on the most important thing, you prioritize based on more primal criteria like recency (What was the latest notification to ping?), fear (Who's the scariest person breathing down your neck?), or comfort (What's the easiest or most fun thing you could strike off your to-do list?). When you make one of these suboptimal prioritization decisions, you dig yourself into a deeper hole. Bad attention choices lead to poor outcomes for your emotions and your energy.

A Better Alternative

What does science tell us about a better alternative?

Most of us work more effectively when we focus on one thing at a time and work uninterrupted for 30 to 45 minutes. Between blocks, we need a 5- or 10-minute rest to reset, and then we're able to do another sprint. After two or three blocks, we need a longer break. One series of studies showed a range in the most productive durations with sprints ranging from 52 to 112 minutes with the accompanying rests of between 17 and 26 minutes. Working this way, in a series of sprints and rests, we get more done, with higher quality, and less stress.

But before you start hacking productivity like a tech bro and thinking that your goal should be 8 (or 18) hours a day of uninterrupted, heads-down focused productivity, note that you're probably built for at most 4 hours a day of this quality of work. Your brain doesn't stay at peak performance for longer than that. In a minute, we'll talk about how you can be ruthless about how you use that prime time, and smart about your hazier focus and more modest productivity the rest of the time.

Another thing to understand about your brain is that different tasks require different brain processes. Task batching (that is, grouping similar activities) reduces the cost of switching and decreases errors. When speed is the goal, put like with like. In contrast, to increase creativity or provide some mental relief, deliberately switch tasks to something with an entirely different vibe.

Armed with that understanding of the value of focus, let's talk about what you can do to reduce your thoughtload by managing your attention.

Chase Outcomes, Not Outputs

Do you go through your week feeling in control? Or does it feel like you're strapped into a theme park ride, being led through corridors of animatronic coworkers repeating the same scripted lines, the monotony broken only by the occasional jump scare? Is it time to take the wheel?

Okay, your work might not be quite like the Pirates of the Caribbean ride, but is it the sanitized corporate version? You're attending the meeting because someone added it to your calendar, responding to the email because it appeared in your inbox, and collating the weekly report because that's how it's always been done.

It's easy to get into a mindless rhythm of going to meetings, responding to emails, and pumping out PowerPoints. The alternative is to be more ruthless (or at least more discerning) about what is worthy of your time and attention. I think of this as figuring out your quest. Yup, from here on out, we're giving you a quest and making you the noble knight who's the hero of the story!

Your quest has three components:

- Activities
- Outputs
- Outcomes

I know, those are boring names. If your work were an adventure story, there might be more exciting descriptors like "trials and tribulations," "conquests," and "ultimate glory," but we're living in the real world here.

Activities refer to the things you do, or the throughputs of work: attending a meeting, building a spreadsheet, conducting research, writing an email, calling a customer, talking to an expert, or drafting a LinkedIn post. Activities are the building blocks of outputs.

Outputs are the things you deliver and the work you get done. Outputs are the finished products: delivering a report, sending an RFP response, rolling out the new feature set, revamping the budget process, submitting a performance management evaluation, or presenting at an industry conference. Outputs are the building blocks of outcomes.

Outcomes are the changes you're creating in the world. The results. The things you can't control directly but are ultimately what determine whether you're successful: a signed contract, a reduced accounts receivable balance, a shift toward higher-priced products, a highly engaged team, an increase in web traffic, a more confident board of directors, or a reduction in clicks on phishing emails.

Obviously, you need all three. The problem arises when you focus on activities and hope that doing enough of them will generate the outputs that will lead to the desired outcomes. That tends not to work.

Here's what I've seen when it comes to your focal point: Focus on activities, become a busy person. Focus on outputs, become a productive person. Focus on outcomes, become an effective person.

Sure, being productive is better than being busy, but if your productivity isn't leading to changes in your outcomes, what's it worth? Being effective is what it's all about. When you pay attention to being effective, you don't need to be as productive because all those things you were churning out that weren't making a dent aren't required anymore. When you don't need to be as productive, you can be less busy because fewer outputs mean fewer tasks. That's the first step in managing your thoughtload—choosing your quest and aligning your attention to accomplish it.

Focus on activities, become busy. Focus on outputs, become productive. Focus on outcomes, become effective.

Noble Quests, Uncomfortable Questions

If you go all in on this thinking, it should throw you for a bit of a loop. When we get too mired in the day-to-day, we forget we're on a noble quest. It's going to take some uncomfortable honesty to admit that you're lost in the woods. If you're doing it right, you should be asking discomfiting questions.

Ask questions about your outcomes: "If that's the most important thing, why have I spent so little time on it lately?" "What would it take to make meaningful progress on that outcome in the next six months?" "Are we on the right quest? Is this what our organization or our customers want, or need?"

Ask questions about your outputs: "How do we know which outputs are driving the outcomes we're looking for?" "Have we had the hard conversation about sunsetting the things that aren't working?" "Does this need to be so exhaustive? If we spent half the time on it, would it deliver the same results?"

Ask questions about your activities: "Why am I spending 50 percent of my time on activities that aren't moving the needle on either outputs or outcomes?" "How do I get out of that standing meeting that's adding zero value?" "Do I really need to go to the retirement party for Stu, who's called me by the wrong name for seven years?"

This was an excruciating exercise for me because it forced me to confront another one of my fails; this one more epic because it had consumed hundreds of hours a year. I was chasing productivity rather than effectiveness. I was enamored of my diligence, hard work, and perseverance for writing a blog post each week for thirteen years and never missing a YouTube upload, but I had lost sight of whether that was the best content and the best distribution approach to achieve the outcomes I strive for.

Are you on the right quest?

I know my outcome—it's the mission statement of our company, 3COze: "Transform the way people communicate, connect, and contribute so they can achieve amazing things together." And when I started creating content in 2012, the outputs I produced furthered that quest. But content creation and consumption have changed fundamentally, and I hadn't kept up. I needed a complete reset in my outputs (and therefore my activities) if I was going to help people achieve amazing things together in the current cluttered, chaotic workplace. With that new clarity, I now achieve more while doing less.

Once it's clear, find a way to keep your quest top of mind. I made a collage of my three most important outcomes and made it my phone's wallpaper; that got my attention! I figured that if I'm going to unlock my device 205 times a day (studies say that's the average), I might as well put something important there.

The work to confront how your environment and even your own delusions direct your attention to all the wrong things can be intense and excruciating. And it's not lost on me that your boss, who is slagging you for not making more progress, is the person most likely to be swamping you with low-value activities. (If that's the case, your boss needs this process as much as you do. Work through it together.)

You have things to accomplish. Real things. Meaningful things. The better defined they are, the easier it is to see what's essential versus what's trivial and wasteful. When you do more of the former and less of the latter, both you and your boss will get kudos. Woo hoo!

Summary: Chase Outcomes, Not Outputs

- **Know the most important outcomes you're trying to create.**
- **Identify the outputs that will drive your desired outcomes.**
- **Emphasize the activities that lead to your high-value outputs.**

Once you know your quest and what will advance it, you'll run headfirst into the next problem . . . *when will it get done*? When will you squeeze in the highest-value activities? That's the next problem we'll solve.

Make Three Priority Lists, Not One

Now that you know what matters most, can you see it reflected in your schedule and your to-do list? Or is your average week spent in service of everyone else's priorities but not your own? Ready to make your schedule serve you?

You open your calendar and see wall-to-wall meetings: the all-hands you can't skip, the monthly business review you attend even though you haven't spoken at it since 2021, and a mysterious invite labeled "Pick your brain" sent by Bob. The work that moves things forward, is it even visible in your 8 a.m. to 5 p.m. calendar view? Or is it hidden out of sight on evenings and weekends? Is your time serving you, or everyone but you?

Most of us have lost all control of time management: the process of aligning our attention with our desired outcomes. Neglecting it is costly because research shows that time management boosts performance by increasing motivation, improving proactiveness, and enhancing creativity.

It also increases job satisfaction, optimism, sense of purpose, and confidence.

But time management doesn't just increase the good stuff; it also reduces distress, including feelings of helplessness and boredom. Time management is a thoughtload triple threat: attention management, emotion management, and energy management all rolled into one. If time management came in pill form, we'd all be taking it.

The most interesting (but least surprising) finding is that the benefits of time management are getting stronger over time. Our dizzying, high thoughtload world needs time management more than ever.

But you won't make headway on time management if you just have one to-do list the length of your arm. To-do lists are terrible for managing your attention (not to mention managing your anxiety or maintaining your energy) because they force you to confront your daunting backlog all in one place, with no help in discerning what to focus on first. The longer your to-do list gets, the more defeated you feel.

Create Three Priority Lists

To start structuring your time to your advantage, you need *three* priority lists, not one to-do list. Think about your priorities in categories.

You already know the Category 1 activities in your time management plan: those tied to your most important outputs and outcomes. What things will you do because they are important to what you are trying to accomplish? Perhaps you will meet with your three largest customers to understand their emerging needs and concerns. Maybe you will attend a project kickoff meeting to ensure your team gets off on the right track. Maybe you shut your door and spend some deep-thinking time designing a product roadmap for the next three years.

Category 1 is the list of activities that are most important to fulfilling your role.

Not all your weekly activities will tie directly to your key outcomes. Category 2 consists of what you do to help others achieve their most significant outcomes. As a field manager, you might attend a cross-functional meeting to provide input on a proposed process. As an account lead, you might write a case study for another team to include in a proposal. As an IT security expert, you might attend a project specification meeting to keep an eye on cyber risk.

Category 2 is the list of activities that other people are counting on you to deliver.

The problem with to-do lists is that they mix critical activities in with mind-numbing hoop-jumping.

Your third list of activities includes the table stakes of being in an organization, such as compliance training, timesheets, and monthly reports. You need to do these because your company needs to comply with laws, impress stakeholders, and remain in business. Even when I'm on a quest to write a book, I still need to send invoices so I can pay the bills and keep the lights on.

Category 3 is the list of activities that just have to get done.

Prioritize Your Priorities

In addition to making you feel like there aren't enough hours in the day, the other problem with to-do lists is that they mix the most critical outcome-driving activities in with the mind-numbing administrative hoop-jumping. You don't want your high thoughtload brain to have to figure out which is which in the heat of the moment. Remember, a brain choked by high thoughtload is terrible at differentiating what's important versus what's trivial.

You have to prioritize.

Even if you ruthlessly pare your three lists down to a handful of items each, that's still way too many activities to be worried about at once. You need to convert long lists into short, prioritized lists—lists with numbers; what's first, second, and third?

So, how do you prioritize your priorities?

Consider these criteria. Is the task

- **important** (an activity that will add value to a key output or outcome)?
- **urgent** (something with growing negative consequences if you wait)?
- **targeted** (a task that no one can do as efficiently or effectively as you)?
- **essential** (core to creating the critical value, not just a nice to have)?

Your top priorities in each category should be based on how important, urgent, targeted, and essential each activity is. One warning: don't over-emphasize urgency. Something important, targeted, and essential might be a better use of your time as a manager than something urgent that you could delegate to someone else.

Trap: Let's pause on that for a sec. How much of your thoughtload comes from doing work that doesn't make sense for you to do, but you do it because you don't want to overburden anyone else, because you haven't had the time to teach someone else how to do it up to your standards, or because it's the easiest way for you to feel useful and you crave the feeling of accomplishment that's harder to come by as a manager?

Ouch. I'm sorry. But you need to be honest with yourself about how much of your thoughtload is there because you choose not to let it go.

A little soul-searching and better prioritization will make a heap of difference. *Psst... Liane... Are you kidding me? I don't have time to make three lists and prioritize everything on them!* (Have we established a telepathic connection, or am I just assuming that's what you were muttering to yourself right about now?)

I get it: When your schedule is out of control, it feels like there's no breathing room to get it under control. The good news is that it doesn't have to take more than a few minutes. And you'll immediately feel the relief of focusing on the right things.

Summary: Make Three Priority Lists, Not One

- **Create three lists: one for your quest, one to help with others', and one for necessary side quests.**
- **Prioritize each list based on how important, urgent, targeted, and essential each task is.**
- **Stick to your unique value as a manager rather than usurping employees' roles.**

You've got the benefit of three prioritized lists, but are the three lists of equivalent value and importance? How do you go from a list to a schedule? Good question.

Schedule in Slots

Do you guard your prime time ruthlessly? Or do you fill the best spots with mindless work and attempt deep work when you're exhausted? Is your schedule making things harder than necessary? If you've solved the "what" and "why," is it time to fix the "when"?

Do you treat Tuesday at 9:00 a.m. exactly the same as Thursday at 4:00 p.m.? Is your project update taking up prime time when it requires about as much processing power as a cat riding a Roomba, while your weekly one-on-one with your most cantankerous employee is on Fridays at 3:00 p.m., when you're 2 hours away from a glass of wine and 1 hour away from a complete meltdown?

There's no point categorizing your tasks if you don't also categorize your time. It's imperative not to let just any activity slide into an available time slot. You need to be deliberate about the value of different real estate on your calendar.

I think of it at three levels.

Focus and Forge Time

This is the most precious time of your week, when your energy is highest, creativity is at its peak, and you're ready for deep work. This is your chance to strike while the iron is hot; and by the iron, I mean the frontal lobe. This is where you schedule your Category 1 activities that advance your agenda, such as writing, researching, or attending important co-creation meetings. (Yes, meetings can be a great use of Focus and Forge time if they are on the right topics, with the right participants and priming. Just don't let this precious real estate get filled with lackluster, low-value meetings.)

The right meetings can be a great use of your most valuable time.

Where are your Focus and Forge slots? Do you have enough of them in your week to accomplish what you want to? And while you've got your calendar open to check, also look at how long they are. Are you attempting to do this kind of work in 30 minutes between meetings? It's not gonna happen. Ideally, based on how human brains work, you want each Focus and Forge chunk to be 2 hours, allowing for two 45-minute blocks with a rest period in between. Don't settle for less than 1-hour chunks. For me, if I can block a whole morning, I feel exhilarated by my work. It's a noticeable difference from a day when I only have an hour or two.

Quick check: Did you open your calendar only to be blinded by a rainbow of meetings squatting on your entire week? Did you immediately jump to the conclusion that Focus and Forge time would need to be relegated to evenings and weekends? If you can't fit 8 hours of this most critical work into your week, you need a reboot. An audience member at a speech laughed when I described Focus and Forge time, admitting she had recently joked to her manager that she would like permission to shift one of her workdays to Saturday because she craved the opportunity to work uninterrupted by meetings and emails. While I implored her not to give up her Saturdays, I did encourage her and her boss to address the problem of too little focus time during the week.

I'll admit to using my fair share of Saturdays to write, but I attempt to protect some real estate Tuesdays through Fridays, from 7 to 11 a.m. That's the spectacular hilltop fortress of my calendar—prime productivity property. Before you send me hate mail, no, I don't get 16 hours of Focus and Forge time during the week; I'm often facilitating or speaking during that time. However, I'm happiest, healthiest, and most productive when I protect at least 8 hours on weekdays for my deep work.

When is your Focus and Forge time? What property does it get on your calendar?

Connect and Collaborate Time

This isn't your prime calendar acreage, but it's the time when you can be relatively efficient and effective. You've got the wherewithal to engage in Category 2 activities such as reviewing someone's work, preparing for an upcoming discussion, or replying to emails that require a thoughtful response. (In part 3, "Restore Your Depleted Energy," we'll talk about how to tap into your natural energy sources to make this time even more effective.)

For me, this slot is in the afternoons from 1:30 to 4:30 p.m. I'm still cogent at that hour but not creative, so it's not a big loss of time for Category 1 activities to progress on my quest. I often do client calls during this time. I'm energized by the conversations at a time when I would be struggling to write or work on my own. But I'm a morning person, so normally, the afternoon is a bit of a lull for me. If your circadian rhythms are different, you might find that protecting some of this time in the mornings before you're revved up makes more sense. Regardless of where it fits on your calendar, you want to protect Connect and Collaborate time to be a good team player and help others on their quests.

Protect time to help your colleagues on their quests.

When is your Connect and Collaborate time? Do you have any Connect and Collaborate activities in the wrong slot at the moment, either clogging up precious time for deep work or relegated to time slots when you don't have the energy or focus to collaborate effectively? How could you change that?

Tidy and Tend Time

The final category is the time when you're one notch above drooling on the desk, and the office goldfish is outdoing you on attention span. This is the deep valley of your calendar real estate where the sun doesn't shine. Perfect! That's where you put Category 3, the keep-the-lights-on activities. Emails. Timesheets. Compliance training. All the side quests. Decide how many hours you will devote to them and put those activities in order from the most important and urgent at the top to the trivial, pencil-pushing, waste-of-time BS at the bottom. Complete as many as possible in the allotted time, then beg forgiveness for the rest. You're doing the most important things, and that's what counts.

One other way to think about your Tidy and Tend time is to squeeze it in between other larger blocks on your calendar. Did a meeting end 10 minutes early? Great, what's on your Category 3 list that could be done in that time? Stuck on hold trying to reach the IT helpdesk? Perfect. You're not going to cure cancer while listening to generic background music and interstitial messages of gratitude for your patience, but you could probably knock off a quick response in the Slack channel.

When is your Tidy and Tend time? Are you letting it eat up too much prime calendar real estate? How could you put a fence around it? Are you being savvy about finding small chunks of Tidy and Tend time in spots that would otherwise be wasted?

Optimizing your time and productivity doesn't mean abandoning all but the most important tasks. It's about what you'll do first in your high-value time and what you'll relegate to the shady valley of your calendar.

Summary: Schedule in Slots

- Define three different time slots: Focus and Forge, Connect and Collaborate, and Tidy and Tend.
- Slot your most important Category 1 activities into Focus and Forge time, Category 2 into Connect and Collaborate, and Category 3 into Tidy and Tend.
- Identify mismatches in your calendar between the work and the time slot, and rearrange where possible.

A well-structured plan for your week can make your thought-load feel much lighter. But a week is so dynamic, and as good as your plan might be, new things will appear on your radar. How do you protect your focus?

Protect Your Focus

Do you end Friday with pride for how you managed your time and how much you accomplished? Or are time bandits luring you off your quest and into the deep, dark woods? Would you like a better way to stay on the path?

Protecting your focus from those who would love to make their priorities into yours is harder than it sounds (and harder than it should be). Interruptions, distractions, and derailers will accost you no matter how optimized your schedule looks on Monday. Protecting your focus requires that you advocate for yourself and know when and how to say no.

Take meetings, for one.

Some meetings are nonnegotiable, but there might be wiggle room with others. Has a meeting worn out its purpose? Could it be deleted, shortened, or held less frequently? Has the chair set the meeting up for success with the right participants or prep work? If not, could it be delayed? Is only some of the content relevant? Could you attend just that part? Reducing meetings is a massive opportunity to protect your time. How many hours could you reclaim for important work if you cut back even 10 percent of your meeting time?

Electronic Disruptions

Never mind the 210 times a day you unlock your phone for a quick peek. There are so many other bings, bleeps, and buzzers vying for your attention. The latest research indicates that the average worker receives a new notification every 2 minutes. Two minutes! How in the world could we not be neurotic?

Which notifications could you turn off?

I allow only two types of notifications to pierce my focus. First, I enable the 10-minute warning before a meeting so I don't get into the flow and blow right past an appointment (although I've been so zoned in that I have missed the start of a meeting more than once).

Second, I leave on my phone ringer so that anyone who wants to reach me can. This strategy works beautifully. For one thing, no one under the age of thirty-five has ever called—it's a wonder they still call it a cell *phone* because none of them use it for that purpose. For another, even Gen Xers have developed a strong aversion to phone calls, so it rings about three times a year. Otherwise, I only see a new email, Slack message, or Notion task when I go looking, but I can work away with the confidence that people *could* reach me if something was urgent.

Many people I know have given up trying to process their email. Some have declared email bankruptcy, while others have learned to live with the little bubble that shows 35,723 unread messages and the constant low-level anxiety that neglecting one of them might turn out to be a career-limiting move. (Yet another example of the thoughtload dilemma showing how your attention choices affect your emotional burden.)

Rather than giving in, how could you think differently about your relationship with your inbox? I found that setting up automation to divert messages such as newsletters from my inbox and directly into folders prevents me from getting distracted by tantalizing new research or a provocative opinion piece in the middle of the day. I know that when my energy is low, I'm vulnerable to delicious distraction. Now I go into that folder when I'm taking a break, instead of falling down the rabbit hole when I'm supposed to be making progress.

Which notifications can you turn off?

You can stay on track in other ways. Pick a few times daily when you'll process email, and keep it closed otherwise. Establish clear standards for electronic communication within your team. It won't fix everything, but it will help you avoid getting sidetracked. I share a variety of tools in the toolkit at thoughtload.com that will help you remove the distractions from your digital world... but what about your environment?

Physical Disruptions

We spend so much time staring at screens and typing into keyboards that we tend to focus on building digital walls while neglecting the importance of physical ones. You might not even have physical walls. My office is just one wall of the kitchen. If you don't have real walls, you'll need to construct virtual walls using materials other than concrete and drywall. A sign on your cubicle. A pair of noise-canceling headphones. I bought a portable screen to put up so my family knows

I'm working, and so I don't have to wash the dishes before a client call. (If you see me on camera, now you know that dinner's detritus is delicately disguised behind the screen.)

Trap: Your instincts and the way you've been socialized might be pointing you in the wrong direction here. As a manager, the "my door is always open" message makes you sound approachable, but it reinforces for the team that prioritization and focus aren't necessary. Instead, model good time and attention boundaries by using effective space boundaries.

Being clear on the highest and best use of your time is a great start, but if you know what you should be accomplishing and still allow others to derail you, you're no better off. Once you make your time serve *your* priorities, not everyone else's, you'll start to feel the momentum. But there's one problem left; we've been talking as if all the distractions and disruptions come from other people. But, as they say in the horror movies, sometimes the call is coming from inside the house.

An open door is an invitation to distraction.

I know, I know! Your desk is covered in a million things, but you know EXACTLY where everything is, right? Well, it turns out that clutter is more of a problem than you think. It adds to your visual field, which requires your brain to use its executive functions to determine what's important. Taxing your frontal lobe that way makes it harder for you to inhibit other intrusions, encode important information, and process what you're working on. (As I write this, I realize I've let my desk get out of hand. Yet another fail. Time to take my own medicine.)

Planning for Disruptions

I'm not suggesting you can avoid all distractions, but you can be better prepared for when they come. Set up a few "if-then" statements so you know what to do when the distraction arises. For example, "If I think of something I have to do, then I'll write it in my planner and get back to my task." If you preset a plan, it will make processing distractions as quick and frictionless as possible.

Speaking of "write it in my planner," I created a tool I call my "Thoughtload Planner." It's part old-school paper agenda and part science-hacked life operating system. I've been using and adapting it for the past five years, and it's made a significant difference to my thoughtload. If you're interested, I've included a link to a downloadable version and the instructions on how to use it in the appendix. This planner has been a lifesaver for me. If you don't already have a system for managing attention, emotions, and energy, you might want to check it out.

Summary: Protect Your Focus

- Reduce time spent on low-value meetings.
- Limit the intrusion of digital notifications and human interruptions.
- Plan for how you'll move on from disruptions when they inevitably happen.

Now you've got a set of attention-focusing techniques that should take the edge off your thoughtload. This is a great foundation to tackle the next factors in thoughtload: emotions and anxiety. So, let's keep going!

When the dragon
is breathing fire,
it's because it's
protecting treasure.

PART 2

Process Your Triggered Emotions

We began chipping away at your thoughtload by focusing your attention, which makes it easier to gain momentum and make meaningful progress. Unfortunately, attention isn't the whole equation. Even if you're focusing intently, emotions can still derail you. Processing your emotions is a crucial component of reducing your thoughtload.

The Achievable Ambition: Calm and Collected

As we did with focusing attention, let's agree on what "good" would look like when it comes to emotions. Although you might be picturing a work environment with no emotions at all, that is neither a realistic nor worthy goal. Emotions are a key part of the human operating system and an important source of information. Instead of eliminating emotions, the goal is to give you greater control of how emotions impact your mood and your productivity. When you know how to process triggered emotions, you can

- distinguish between what to worry about and what not to,
- translate from feelings to facts to action,
- see options in situations where you might otherwise have reacted impulsively,
- keep conflicts focused on the issues rather than making them personal, and
- feel more emotionally available because you're not trying to keep it together.

Science Synopsis

Like with distracted attention, the experience of triggered emotions comes from a combination of what you're exposed to and how you process it.

While we often use the words "feeling" and "emotion" interchangeably, they are different processes. Emotions are complex, patterned collections of chemical, neural, and physiological responses triggered by internal or external stimuli. Put more simply, emotions are what happens in your body when your senses pick up something noteworthy.

The important thing to know is that most of the action in an emotion is preconscious; you're not in control of it.

Feelings, on the other hand, are the mental representation of the physiological emotion. Feelings are the stories we tell ourselves to rationalize the emotions we're experiencing. For example, if your heart is racing and your palms are sweating as you wait to give a presentation, you might call it nervousness and justify it because the audience is judging you. Unlike emotions, feelings are conscious, cognitive processes.

When you notice and appreciate the difference between emotions and feelings, you can interrupt the default narrative and choose a more constructive story. You will find out how in this part.

Like all higher-order animals, humans have an emotional system that evolved to keep us safe; one that creates an early warning system when something is amiss and directs our bodies to prepare for action. Now, if you're a zebra, this system is finely tuned to detect a predator and move your legs fast enough to avoid becoming lunch. But you're not a zebra, and your ancestors didn't survive by being faster or having better camouflage.

Instead, humans' evolutionary advantage comes from our social relationships. We cooperated to survive. Because of the importance of our social connections to our safety, our emotional state and perceptions of threat are closely tied to our status in the group. Do I belong? Will I be protected? Getting voted out of the cave (or off the island) meant you got eliminated from the gene pool.

Now apply that to the workplace. Imagine the primal paranoia in a typical team meeting. Am I in or out? Do my colleagues value me, or are they undermining me? Will they disown me for reheating fish in the microwave? (BTW, the answer to that last one is, "Yes, undoubtedly, yes." Don't do it.)

Given the importance of inclusivity, it makes sense that humans experience social pain—the aversive sensation that accompanies the perception of being excluded from a group. Social pain might be caused by being left out of a conversation, being criticized, or getting signals that you're not valued. Are you now realizing why your interactions and meetings might seem more emotional than warranted by the less-than-scintillating subject matter?

Trap: Many managers discount social pain and how aversive these team dynamics can be. I promise you that issuing a quarterly reminder that "it's business, not personal" will not make a dent in the problem (but will make a dent in trust and engagement scores). Social pain is real and physiological. Various studies have demonstrated that our brains experience social pain similarly to physical pain; the same brain networks are activated in both processes. Who knew the colloquial expression "that hurt my feelings" is physiologically apt?

You really can hurt someone's feelings.

To add more evidence to the idea that social pain is a real pain, one of my colleagues published research showing that acetaminophen can reduce perceptions of social pain, just as it helps alleviate aching muscles or throbbing wounds. (Are you thinking what I'm thinking? There are a couple of meetings this week that could benefit from a couple of Tylenol...)

So you have all the ingredients for highly emotional individuals. Now, let's talk about how emotions from one person create a frenzy of feelings among the whole team.

Emotional contagion is the unconscious transfer of one person's emotional state to another person. Emotions spread as invisibly and as potently as airborne viruses. The process occurs when a transmitter's behaviors (their expressions, words, pitch, tone, and gestures) infect a receiver, causing the receiver's mood to shift. Ultimately, the two people's emotions converge.

Think of it this way: Your colleague is sad, which shows up in slumped shoulders, downcast eyes, a drooping frown, and shrinking pupils. (Pupil dilation seems especially important to emotional contagion.) Your brain processes these gestures and, without knowing it, you begin to mimic them. As your body language, tone, and expressions deflate, your brain interprets these physical symptoms as signs that you feel sad, too.

You can think of emotional contagion as a mood sandwich.

Their Mood > Their Behavior > Your Behavior > Your Mood

To be fair, I'm focusing on the spread of unpleasant emotions because they are the biggest issue for thoughtload, but emotional contagion can be negative or positive. As a manager, you need to understand and harness both. We'll delve into the techniques for doing that in part 5.

One important note: Emotional contagion is *not* the same as empathy. When you empathize with someone, you understand their feelings without experiencing them. Empathy is a cognitive process. Emotional contagion, in contrast, happens without your awareness. It is sympathy, "feeling with," whereas empathy is "feeling for" another person. If you're going to manage your thoughtload and give yourself a chance of being helpful to someone in distress, you don't want to be overcome by the same emotions. You want to promote empathy and guard against sympathy.

Phew, a *lot* is going on around the table. If science has us taking emotions much more seriously, what does it tell us about the hope of wrangling them?

Emotional Regulation and Dysregulation

Emotional dysregulation is the state where individuals struggle to control the intensity, duration, and expression of their emotions. That includes poor impulse control, emotional outbursts, and rapid or severe mood swings. While some individuals are more emotionally reactive than others, dysregulation can happen to any of us in stressful situations or when we're exhausted (hello again, treacherous triad of thoughtload). At work, emotional dysregulation manifests in various forms, including angry outbursts, welled-up tears, mean-spirited comments, prolonged venting, and impulsive behaviors.

The good news is that you can learn to navigate a constructive path through emotional experiences, starting with awareness of what's happening and then drawing on emotional regulation techniques. These will ground you in the situation, reframe your thinking, and move you toward action. Research suggests that becoming more aware and comfortable with emotions alone, even without taking any additional steps, can reduce reactiveness. Once you apply emotional regulation techniques, you realize the benefits they offer to well-being and overall success. Let's get into some approaches you can use to process your emotions.

Interrupt Your Feelings

Are you wise to the fact that the narrator in your head often serves you fiction? Or do you buy what the little voice is selling you every time? Would you like to learn how to put that nasty narrator in its place?

Feeling a little queasy before a big presentation? It's probably because the folks from sales are hoping you'll fall flat on your face. Yelling in a meeting, what choice did you have? There is *no sense of urgency around here!* Are your emotions spinning up into feelings and stories that are doing you a disservice?

When you recognize that your emotions set off a cascade of feelings, stories, and rationalizations that can hijack you, you're in a much better position to interrupt the process. The key is to realize, as Susan David says, "Emotions are data, not directives."

Begin to interrogate your emotions and interrupt your feelings, ideally by practicing with innocuous emotions in a safe setting. What happens when you watch your favorite sports team trailing with 2 minutes to go? Or when you're reading an engrossing novel or reacting to a radio call-in show during your commute? Work up to more substantive emotions and higher-stakes situations. When you feel the emotion, take these five steps: catch it, locate it, express it, assess it, and release it.

Five Steps to Process Emotional Reactions

First things first. Recognize you're having an emotional reaction. It sounds silly, but when you're focused on being productive, persuasive, or profound, you're more aware of what's going on in your mind and less attuned to what's happening in your body. You ignore the signals of interoception (the internal equivalent of sight or taste, where your brain registers signals from your organs and muscles). The result is disembodiment (kind of like the science fiction talking head in the jar). Failing to catch on to what's happening in your body is a major cause of emotional dysregulation.

Don't focus on your thoughts and lose sight of what's happening in your body.

To improve your emotional regulation, reconnect your mind to your body. You need the information it's providing. So you locate it, pinpointing where the emotion is manifesting in your body. It might be churning, nausea, or butterflies in your gut. Or changes to your heart rate and breathing. Your skin is also a giant canvas that reveals your emotions as you blush, turn pale, or feel the hairs on the back of your neck stand up.

Focusing on where the emotion shows up in your body creates some mental distance from it. With practice, you can even begin to control those reactions that most of us think are beyond our control. Adding some form of mindfulness or meditation can help.

Once you've spent a few seconds focused on *where* the emotion is showing up, express it. Which emotion is it? How would you label the experience you're having? You can start with the basics—anger, sadness, fear, disgust, and joy—you know, the Pixar's *Inside Out* characters. Don't stop there. If your racing heart, clenched jaw, and sweaty palms tell you you're angry, is that anger in the form of frustration, annoyance, dismissiveness, or something else? The labels that work best are specific and granular. When you're clear about exactly what you're feeling, you're more equipped and more likely to use strategies to regulate that emotion.

The key is not to accept the first story you tell yourself about why you're experiencing what you're experiencing. You must assess the veracity and the value of the story you're telling yourself. Imagine a scenario where your boss walks into the room and makes a beeline for your colleague. She lavishes praise on him for his amazing project work. You immediately feel anger, which you recognize as jealousy. You worked as hard on that as he did. She's playing favorites.

Now, ask yourself, is your story true? Maybe, if you give her a minute to walk farther into the room, you'll get the same praise. And even if the boss has no intention of talking to you, is feeling jealous helpful? Is that how you want to feel? If not, tell yourself a different story, like, "I'm glad he's getting some attention; he's new and still building his credibility."

This one took me a *long* time. I often narrated my story as, "You made me angry," or "You hurt my feelings." This was especially true at home. Last winter, we had a massive snowstorm. It came down for three days, which was especially problematic because we have a 70-foot-long driveway. Early in the storm, one of our two shovels broke under the weight of the wet snow. With only one shovel left, we took turns going out every couple of hours to try to keep up with the accumulation. During one of my turns, Craig, my husband, took the shovel and started clearing. What did I do? I cried, of course. (Can't relate? You would have been thrilled for a break?) I was hurt and offended. He clearly thought I wasn't up to the job; not worthy, some fragile woman. Oh yeah, I whipped it into a juicy story about how he was being condescending and unappreciative; how *he* was the villain. (I promised you that I fail at this stuff all the time!) Thankfully, I realized the fiction I was creating and admitted to Craig what I was feeling. It was all over in a matter of minutes, but only because doing this work has made me keenly aware of what's going on. Earlier in our marriage, the same situation would have led to a 3-day silent treatment where I punished him for a crime he didn't know he committed.

This. Is. Huge! Most days, I now make better choices about how I want to feel. (Most days.)

Emotional experiences aren't optional, but the narratives you wrap around them are. It's your story, you choose.

The secret to better emotional regulation is to change the questions you ask and the order in which you ask them. Instead of immediately jumping to why you're feeling something and who's to blame, start with where you're experiencing it, then what you're feeling, then consider why. As you take ownership of your emotional cascade, you'll realize that the most important who in the equation is you.

Once you're aware of what's going on in your body and mind and in control of the narrative, you can release the emotions. Leave them behind and find a path to action. Choose one thing that will allow you to get on with your day.

That could be an act that addresses the root cause of the feeling. In our jealousy example, you could walk up to the boss and your colleague and chime in with your congratulations as well. Alternatively, you could do something to change the vibe, like striking up a conversation with someone else in the room on a completely different topic. Either way, you've learned what you can from the emotion, and you're moving on.

Emotions Happen

Let me pause and say that processing an emotion and then moving past it is different from pretending it didn't happen. Ignoring, repressing, or denying your negative emotions can seriously affect your mental and physical health. Fighting against negative thoughts can make them stronger and more intrusive, and allow them to stay around longer. (Although some emerging research runs counter to the conventional wisdom and suggests that suppressing some types of troubling thoughts might be beneficial.) All that to say, don't skip the catching, locating, expressing, and assessing, and go straight to repressing instead of releasing.

Summary: Interrupt Your Feelings

- Recognize the difference between an emotional experience and the feelings you use to explain it.
- Learn to process emotions by catching, locating, expressing, assessing, and then releasing them.
- Choose a narrative that gives you a path toward constructive action.

Learning to spot, interrogate, and interrupt your emotions puts you in control, but it requires considerable energy. When your thoughtload is high, and your quest daunting, you might be less of a noble knight and more of a fire-breathing dragon. That's what we'll tackle next.

Know Your Treasure

Are you calm about even the most sensitive issues? Or do some topics trigger an emotional reaction? When stressed, do your feelings throw you for a loop? Would you like a way to better manage your triggers?

We've already introduced the idea of you as a brave knight on a noble quest. Well, every noble quest has a fire-breathing dragon, right? That dragon breathes fire when someone gets too close to their treasure.

We don't get emotional over every little thing; we get emotional because we feel that something that matters to us is threatened. This process typically plays out in a pattern:

- Your senses tell you a marauder is approaching.
- Your emotions tell you that you're afraid.
- Your feelings convince you the marauder is coming to steal your treasure.

When you know what your treasure is and how to properly safeguard it, you're less likely to be taken off guard by someone encroaching. You're better positioned to choose a deliberate and rational response rather than an emotional one.

So, what's your treasure? Do you have a sense of the things that matter deeply to you? Can you name them without thinking twice? Is your treasure feeling included? Or being the expert in the room? Or your relationships with key customers?

You might have ready access to these values, beliefs, or motives. What comes to mind? What are the things that matter to you at work that might be enough to trigger an emotional reaction if you perceive they are being threatened? Although you probably have a sense of some of your hot buttons, you might be completely unaware of others. As Dr. Tasha Eurich's research demonstrates, you're probably not as self-aware as you think you are. You have work to do to map your buried treasure.

Reflection

The simplest way to uncover your treasure is to reflect on situations where you've become emotional, particularly on what consistently irritates or upsets you. When was the last time you felt frustrated, insecure, infuriated, or judgmental at work? What was going on? What story did you tell yourself? What made it feel unsafe or threatening?

Ask yourself, "Why does this bother me?" Don't stop at the first answer—keep asking "why" until you get to a deeper belief or need. This simple process, sometimes called a "why chain," helps move from surface-level annoyances to the core values or expectations driving your reaction.

My colleague, Matt, had a great example of this. Matt runs the agency I work with on all my content. Recently, I sent him a document I created using AI that was full of ideas about how to market this book. Matt reacted emotionally and felt dismissive of the value of what I'd sent. Upon reflection, he realized that it was less about the quality of the ideas and more about feeling excluded from idea generation. Matt's treasure is being a strategic partner, not just an execution coordinator. He was telling himself a story about being superfluous and no longer needed. This was so far from the truth. Matt often feels like an extra lobe in my brain. We talked through a different version of the story in which I wasn't serving up a finished meal; I was sending him ingredients and inviting him to cook with me. Now that we both know where Matt's treasure is buried, we're more aware of the issue and better positioned to talk openly and rationally about when and how I involve him.

Follow the "why chain" to identify what matters deeply to you.

What's your treasure? For example, if you get frustrated when meetings run long, consider why. Maybe because it throws off the rest of your day. Why does that matter? Because it leaves you feeling rushed and behind. Why is that important? Because being organized and in control is what helps you remain calm and effective. What's so important about being calm and effective? Yada, yada. Keep going until you land on something that feels essential not only to how you function at work but fundamental to who you are. That's your treasure.

Reflect on a few scenarios and see if a pattern emerges. Do you need to feel in control and, therefore, react anxiously to surprises or setbacks? Do you need to feel respected and respond angrily to situations or people who question your status? Do you have high standards for yourself and experience overwhelm and discouragement if you don't make enough progress? There are no right answers here (and no judgment), but the important thing is to know what you're protecting so you can be better prepared and more in control.

Friends, colleagues, and family members can be excellent sources as you chart your treasure map. After all, they see you in action and can observe your facial expressions, register your body language, and note changes in your tone more readily than you can. (I love the expression, "You can't see the label from inside the jar.")

Ask them what territory feels too tender to tread on with you. Which topics do they tiptoe around? Are there issues they avoid because of how you'll react? You can try questions like, "In what situations do I over-apply my strengths?" "What are my blind spots?" or "When do I turn from Dr. Jekyll into Mr. Hyde?" You don't have to agree with what they see on the surface, but I guarantee you it's a good place to start digging.

Your colleagues will likely have valuable insight about when you pick up an issue, put tension on a discussion, or disagree vehemently. You can learn a lot about your treasure based on the things you're willing to fight for and those you aren't.

Assessment

When we do team effectiveness work at my company, 3COze, we administer an assessment tool that identifies people's underlying needs and beliefs. This tool differs from the more superficial style tools that focus on how you behave or what you like; this one gets to what environment you need to feel calm, cool, and collected. Essentially, it tells you your treasure.

To grossly oversimplify, it differentiates between people based on what they need to stay grounded:

- Those who need action
- Those who need influence
- Those who need possibility
- Those who need predictability

An assessment can help you understand why some situations feel threatening and give you the insight to adapt your environment in ways that mean you're triggered less often. Using an assessment tool is also a great exercise to do with your team.

One leader we used the assessment tool with, Anna, turned out to value predictability and fairness strongly. Anything that changed the plan, bent the rules, or advantaged one group or another would cause Anna to go from the kindest, most mild-mannered team player into a stone-faced crusader for justice. The transformation was immediate and alarming. She had one particularly obvious tell that she felt threatened; she would start using the word "should" repeatedly. "You *should* do it this way." "It *shouldn't* have happened." "We *should've* done something different." I suggested she was "shoulding all over people," which, when you say it, sounds a lot like another expression that is equally applicable. As she became more aware of her need for predictability and fairness, she could be more proactive about issues to avoid being caught off guard. In cases where something triggered her sense of injustice in the moment, she learned to catch herself mid-shoulding and redirect her emotional reaction into constructive questions about a plan's intent, its unintended consequences, and better alternatives. Once she understood where her reactions were coming from, she felt less stressed and better able to deal with her feelings without going on the attack.

Doing the work to uncover your treasure makes you more aware of situations that might trigger you, better able to access options for what to think and feel, and less likely to turn into the fire-breathing dragon.

Summary: Know Your Treasure

- Recognize that emotional reactions are more likely when the issue is important.
- Reflect on what matters most to you and what happens when it feels threatened.
- Seek additional input about your treasure from colleagues, friends, family, and assessment tools.

Knowing your treasure is usually enough to keep you calm and rational. But occasionally, you'll lose your cool. What happens if your emotions get the better of you? It doesn't have to be a career-limiting move. Let's talk about how to handle it well.

Pair Vulnerability with Accountability

When your emotions run hot, do you recover quickly? Or do you lose time, trust, and respect, turning a 5-second flare-up into a 3-act saga? Would you love to be able to move on quicker after an emotional flare-up?

The desire to avoid emotions is a mistake, but sadly, one that's embedded in the antiquated culture of most businesses. I feel frustrated that our messages to managers convey the impression that you always have to be strong, rational, and on top of things. While I believe that you need to take ownership of your feelings and build your emotional regulation skills, I'm disheartened when I speak with managers who tell me that they can't show emotion because doing so would be a career-limiting move. (Of course, I'm even more irate that in some organizations, they're right.)

Protecting against any and all negative emotions requires heavy armor and leads to three significant problems. First, while your emotional armor might make you feel impenetrable, it requires tremendous energy to carry it. We're trying to reduce the load here, not make everything feel heavier. Second, if you create armor strong enough to stop any emotions from getting out, it will also stop any from getting in. That's self-defeating because a manager who appears dispassionate also seems disconnected. Your team needs to know that you care about the work and about them. If you're too restrained, they won't feel confident in your personal investment in them. Third, donning emotional armor and projecting invincibility sends the message that your team members need to wear armor and be invincible too. If you don't show emotion, how do they know it's okay for them to? The best part of an occasional emotional outburst is showing everyone you've got a dragon too.

Share Your Struggles and Your Thinking

Being transparent about your challenges can humanize you and improve the emotional literacy of the team. For example, if you've tried three different approaches to convince your boss you need more funding, sharing with your team that you're frustrated you haven't landed on a compelling way to defend your case yet is worthwhile. Alternatively, if you're fighting distraction and distress because your mom is in the hospital this week, tell your team so they know it's not about them, and so they can have your back. (It's not a hypothetical situation. I delivered a full day of leadership training while my mom was having triple bypass surgery because we both agreed that it would be better than me sitting in a waiting

Protecting against emotions requires heavy armor.

room, freaking out. Coincidentally, the audience was a group of physician leaders, so when I told them what was going on, they were reassuring. Mom came through like a champ, and I felt a special connection to my co-facilitator and that cohort of leaders who were so supportive of me when I was vulnerable.)

I'm a strong advocate of showing a little vulnerability in the service of authenticity, empathy, and connection. However, vulnerability from a leader can erode confidence unless it's tied to strong accountability. We look to those with power or status to figure out how we should feel. If an employee looks into your eyes and all they see is fear, confusion, or surrender, they're going to get a whole lot more nervous. Instead, when you're working through an emotional experience, demonstrate that you're actively managing it, even if you're still struggling.

If you're having an emotional reaction and trying to hide it from your team, your elaborate ruse is probably not working. It's a lot like when you came home drunk in high school, pretending you were sober and convinced that you'd done an ace job fooling your parents. You're kidding yourself. They know. Remember that your pupils are important in transmitting emotional information; that's gonna be hard to fake.

Instead of trying to suppress your emotions, narrate your traitorous face. "I'm stuck and worrying about how this will sound to our long-time customers." Or, "Sorry, I'm still three comments back, feeling demoralized by what Sean said." Taking ownership of your emotional reactions, even if it's just a wayward eyebrow, goes a long way in demonstrating your authenticity to your team and modeling healthy emotional regulation.

Focus On Forward

Sharing is good, but your team doesn't want to get stuck in a drama cycle any more than you do. One of my favorite clients says, "It's okay to visit Pity City; just don't buy real estate." That means your job is to get back on the road; ideally, recommitted to your quest. Articulate a next step that will move you past the emotional moment and on to an action that will change things for the better.

If you're fretting about how the new pricing will land with your customers, agree that each team member will have a conversation with three clients and then report back their reactions. Or, ask your fantastic communications person to draft the messaging to position the price change. Action is the antidote to anxiety.

You think they don't know. They know.

I saw a manager do a great job of this when a project his team had been working on for three months was in peril due to a cost-cutting initiative. He was trying to be objective and contribute to the best decision for the business overall, but he couldn't help feeling that his team would be crushed, not to mention that they'd lose faith in him as their advocate. Once he admitted as much to everyone in the room, he was able to manage his emotions and support his boss, who decided that his program would, in fact, be the one to go. The manager needed to take a positive step forward, so he asked his boss for help communicating that his team was still highly valued by the organization. He was more than happy to oblige.

Take Responsibility

Occasionally, your emotions might come through in a way that you're not proud of. Your fire-breathing dragon might scorch someone. In that case, be sure to provide a strong apology that includes what you did, the impact of your choices, and what you'll do to ensure it doesn't happen again. You need all three of these components for an apology to repair the damage.

An apology without vulnerability comes off as callous and robotic. Conversely, if you overemphasize vulnerability without accountability, such as dwelling on how terrible you feel without specifying what you'll do differently next time, people will lose confidence in you. Either way, your integrity takes a hit, and once it's gone, it's exceptionally difficult to earn back.

Employees pay close attention to how people in positions of authority handle sensitive situations. When a manager takes responsibility for their emotional reactions without flinching, overexplaining, or shifting blame, it sets a powerful precedent. The first time you admit that you were emotional, misjudged something, or overreacted—and then describe what you're going to do to make it right—you send a signal: This is what leadership looks like.

If you dodge, deflect, or gloss over your reaction, the lesson is clear: Appearances matter more than integrity. That's how cultures of self-protection, blame, and risk aversion take root.

When you model vulnerability wrapped in personal accountability, it gives others the permission and the language to do it too. You normalize candor. You humanize work. And most importantly, you remove the unrealistic pressure of trying to be unemotional from your thoughtload and everyone else's.

Summary: Pair Vulnerability with Accountability

- Admit vulnerability when you're feeling it rather than trying to disguise it.
- Pair vulnerability with accountability to bolster connection without eroding confidence.
- Apologize when necessary by expressing what you did, its impact, and what you'll do differently in the future.

When you've got the energy to use these approaches, they work. But sometimes, you're barely keeping it together, and you simply cannot give yourself grace in the face of an emotional reaction. That's when you need a side-door strategy.

Give to Get

Are you gracious with yourself in emotional moments, or are you a ruthless critic who layers new distress on top of the original? Is it time to be as kind to yourself as you are to everyone else?

This final thought about how to process your emotions to manage your thoughtload is a bit counterintuitive.

As we've discussed, one of the most effective approaches for coping with difficult situations is to interrogate your emotions and interrupt your feelings. The secret is to reframe the situation into a more positive and constructive narrative. Can we be real for a minute? When you're at your wits' end, feeling frantic, demoralized, or defeated, positive thinking and healthy reframing can be in short supply. It's a big ask.

In that case, stop trying to fix yourself and start trying to be of service to someone else. It turns out that one way to increase the likelihood that you'll give yourself grace is to give it to someone else first. And better yet, being empathetic and coaching someone on ways to reframe their unhealthy narratives into something constructive has been shown to build your skills and increase the likelihood that you'll reframe your own negative feelings. Help you, help me.

Learning by Teaching

I'm laughing because I sometimes say something in a speech and have a mini out-of-body experience where a little version of me floats out, wags a finger back at me, and says, *super*-judgmentally, "Mm, hmm . . . Maybe we should try that ourselves, hmm?" As I'm teaching the concept, I'm simultaneously learning and reinforcing it for myself. That's what this method is all about—learning through teaching.

To try it, look for opportunities to speak with someone who is struggling. (I can assure you it's not hard to find them these days.) This could be a member of your team, a colleague, a friend, or a loved one. For the purposes of improving your emotional regulation, whom you're speaking with is less relevant than how you're helping them.

Often, opportunities to help people make sense of their feelings will arise naturally in conversation—that is, if you show people you're not in a rush and that you're fully present with them. (Like always, attention matters.) Once someone has opened the door to a topic they're upset about, you can encourage candor with questions such as, "What's not coming as easily as you'd like?" "What's unpleasant about that situation?" "How are you feeling about that?" (Craig taught me a trick: If you're trying to get a stoic or guarded person to open up about their feelings, ask them how they're *thinking* about the issue rather than how they're *feeling*. It doesn't change the answer, it just makes them less squeamish about sharing.)

As the person divulges something they're struggling with, acknowledge their negative experience, validate their emotions, and express empathy for what they're going through. For example, the person might say, "I'm struggling to connect with Glen. I feel like he doesn't respect me." Your first response could be as simple as saying, "That sounds really rough," or "I'm sorry things are off to a slow start." Another helpful addition is to normalize their experience by saying something like, "Interpersonal dynamics on teams can be so challenging," or "It can take time to forge a new relationship." As you share encouraging and empathetic words with the other person, your brain listens and learns that you could be kinder to yourself, too.

Ask how people are thinking rather than how they're feeling.

Now we've got the empathy bit down, the second component of emotional regulation is to reappraise the situation. Based on what they've told you, ask questions to encourage them to look at things from a different angle: "How do you think Glen is feeling about this?" "What might he be trying to achieve by saying that?" "How else could you interpret his comments?" Alternatively, offer your own perspective: "I think Glen was keen to prove his worth and might have interjected to impress us, rather than to disparage you."

As you suggest alternative explanations or different ways to think or feel about the situation, you demonstrate that there are myriad possibilities for what Glen intended or why the situation played out as it did. You model cognitive flexibility and a healthy mistrust of the default stories that we tell ourselves. Somewhere deep in your brain, you register that the same applies to the fiction you feed yourself.

After you get in a few reps of helping others to practice self-acceptance, reframing, and emotional regulation, you'll start to improve at these skills yourself. This is like a dream scenario where you're the physical trainer and you get fit while the client does the sit-ups. How awesome is that?

In more good news, these conversations don't even need to be in person. They don't even have to be conversations. The study I'm referring to used an online forum where participants supported one another while interacting asynchronously via text messaging. While research suggests that phone conversations are best for forging a strong connection and demonstrating empathy, modeling emotional regulation, even in a sparse medium like texting, can make you both feel better.

Coach Yourself

Once you've practiced coaching others to reframe their feelings into more constructive narratives, you can try doing it for yourself. When you hear yourself say, "I can't believe I messed that up. I'm such an idiot!" pause and think of what you would say to a colleague in this moment. Odds are, you'd respond with something more like, "Everyone makes mistakes—what matters is how you recover."

This isn't about toxic positivity or pretending things are fine. It's about being kind to yourself. If you wouldn't let someone else beat themselves up over a small error or a tough day, why would it be okay to do it to yourself? Over time, this practice becomes a habit and strengthens emotional regulation by interrupting harsh, spiraling thoughts with a more measured, supportive narrative.

Practicing reverse empathy takes intention. It might start with writing a few phrases down, using them in a journal, or even saying them aloud. But once you build the muscle, you'll find it easier to reframe, refocus, and get back on track.

Like I said in the introduction to "Interrupt Your Feelings," the idea isn't to deny or diminish your emotions, because emotions are at the core of the human operating system. The goal is to have greater control of how you use them and the valuable information they provide.

Emotions are at the core of the human operating system.

Having created a gap between your emotions and your feelings, figured out your treasure and your triggers, accepted that you can be vulnerable and accountable at the same time, and boosted your mood by helping others, you may find your emotions are much more of an asset than a liability.

Summary: Give to Get

- When you're struggling to regulate your own emotions, help someone regulate theirs.
- Express empathy for their experience, and then help them reappraise the situation.
- Talk yourself through your own emotional reactions by imagining you're coaching a friend.

Alright, you're making progress. You've got a set of attention-focusing techniques and approaches for processing your emotions. That will help you make a major dent in your thoughtload. One more step: Time to boost your energy so that the thoughtload feels even lighter to carry.

Get your energy
from both waterfalls
and wells.

PART 3

Restore Your Depleted Energy

Now it will become abundantly clear why energy is the final pillar in reducing your thoughtload. Everything you've learned about focusing your attention and processing your emotions is a necessary starting point for restoring your energy. If your thoughts are racing and your heart is pounding, your energy burn rate will be too high to keep up. Now that we've addressed both factors in the numerator of the thoughtload equation, let's consider the denominator: the energy you have to carry the load.

Achievable Ambition: Recharged and Resilient

What's the ideal state when it comes to energy use? It's not zero. In the introduction to the previous part on emotions, we talked about how the goal is not to eliminate emotions altogether. Likewise here, the idea is not to minimize the energy you spend. You're on a quest; you've got important things to accomplish. The goal is to have reliable and renewable power sources that you can tap into for all the energy you need to do the things that matter. That means you

- feel motivated enough to invest in the activities that make you feel better,
- sustain your attention for extended periods,
- forgo the quick-fix energy hits in favor of longer-lasting energy boosts,
- experience moments of joy and lightheartedness throughout the week, and
- have the energy to make the better choice rather than the most expedient one.

That's a long way from what I'm seeing in organizations these days.

Science Synopsis

Energy is a dynamic system with diverse puts and takes. So, before we get into strategies to help you improve your energy balance sheet, let's talk about the factors that affect your physical, mental, and emotional energy.

Your body is an amazing metabolic machine that converts food into energy to maintain normal bodily functions and conduct regular repair. To ensure you have enough energy to make it to your next meal (and a little extra in reserve in case you encounter a sabertooth tiger), your body is constantly recalibrating to operate in the cheapest way possible. And it's not always transparent about what it's up to. It turns out that your brain signals you're tired and it's time to slow down long before your body is physically depleted. Your miserly brain is doing all it can to conserve energy. Knowing that your brain is trying to trick you into being lazy helps you realize there's more in the tank than you might think.

The optimal way to renew your energy is in cycles of work and rest. While the stress of high expectations and a barrage of demands make it tempting to "push through," it's not the best approach because your energy and your output flag over time. The issue is that your brain, particularly your prefrontal cortex (the part of your brain responsible for what's referred to as "executive functioning," such as deciphering, deciding, and inhibiting), becomes fatigued with use.

The science is still emerging, but several factors likely contribute to cognitive fatigue. First, your brain needs glucose to function. In the case of the prefrontal cortex, it requires a lot of it. Your body can only deliver so much glucose in a fixed period. When it runs low, you'll notice a drop in your ability to focus, make decisions, and exercise self-control. Another component of fatigue appears to stem from the buildup of glutamate, a waste product. You don't need to know all the mechanisms (a good thing, since even neuroscientists are still trying to figure them out); you just need to understand that it all adds up to the phenomenon of ultradian cycles, where your energy peaks and wanes over a cycle that can be as short as 10 minutes or up to a few hours.

You won't be surprised to learn that the higher the cognitive demands, the quicker the energy drain. Paying attention to too many things or engaging in strenuous mental activity accelerates cognitive fatigue. That, and of course, emotional burdens, anxiety, and stress, also wear you out more quickly. Another reminder that if you don't tackle the top of the thoughtload equation, you won't be able to make headway on the bottom.

The critical takeaway is that you need to eat food with protein and complex carbohydrates that provide a steady stream of energy (rather than creating peaks and valleys) and take 10- to 15-minute breaks that give your brain time to recharge. Don't let your brain run out of fuel, or you'll be coasting through situations that need your foot on the gas.

Emotional Energy

Sometimes your energy level isn't about whether your body is fueled and ready, nor is it about whether your mind is in peak form; sometimes your energy is more closely tied to your motivation. Consider a time when you were well rested and ready to go, but the first thing on your calendar was a mind-numbing meeting where you were rehashing and relitigating topics you'd already reheated multiple times. It's probably about as appetizing as the cafeteria serving up the same chicken and beans the third day in a row—this time disguised in burrito form.

Motivation is critical to your energy and essential for reducing the perceived weight of your thoughtload. But not all motivation is created equal. Intrinsic motivation, the kind that comes from curiosity, interests, or the opportunity for personal growth, is a renewable energy source. When you've got strong internal motivation, you can carry a heavy load longer without wearing out.

In contrast, extrinsic motivation, which is the drive to accomplish things that will bring you valuable rewards or help you avoid aversive consequences, can provide a quick hit of energy, but it's less sustainable. Some organizations use extrinsic motivators, such as bonus payments, incentives, and the fear of being chastised to coerce the behaviors they're looking for. That approach to motivating people can make the load feel much heavier.

Intrinsic motivation reduces the weight of your thoughtload.

Restoring energy isn't just about sleeping or resting; it's about reconnecting with what motivates you.

Physical and Mental Energy

Although it might sound counterintuitive, one of the most effective ways to boost your energy is through physical activity. Getting your heart rate up and your body moving is a great way to increase blood flow and deliver more oxygen and glucose to your brain. The benefits are even greater in the long term, as exercise reduces inflammation and stress, improves sleep, and enhances cognitive function. Ah, look at that—attention, emotions, and energy together again. Exercise is another killer app for reducing thoughtload.

While jumping on the treadmill might be practical, the energy benefits of exercise are even higher if you get your movement outside (although I often settle for basement exercise myself). There's plenty of evidence that time spent in nature adds to the benefit of movement, and if that nature includes a view of water, you'll also get the bonus of lowered blood pressure. Neil Pasricha wrote a compelling piece about bird-watching—"8 Reasons Why It's Time to Become a Birdwatcher"—to manage stress and boost your energy. I'm giving it a try.

One last important factor: Your nervous system has two opposing modes. When your brain perceives your environment as safe and predictable, you experience parasympathetic activity where your body aims to "rest and digest." In contrast, when something triggers your brain's stress response, the sympathetic mode prepares your body to protect you. This leads to an increased heart rate, greater alertness, and a short-term energy boost. Those of us who love a deadline often take advantage of that to push work across the finish line.

Exercise is a killer app for reducing thoughtload.

The problem comes when you are in that stress mode too often or for too long. In such cases, your body continually releases neurotransmitters and hormones, such as adrenaline and cortisol, which are typically reserved for acute situations. The prolonged presence of these chemicals in your body can damage your health, deplete your energy, and make you more error-prone.

You don't need to understand the highly complex mechanisms; you just need to focus on balancing the two states. Once you reset into parasympathetic mode to rest and recover, you can benefit from the sympathetic activity and the helpful form of stress that energizes you when you've got something important or urgent to do. We'll get into a few techniques for rebalancing your energy levels next.

Find Flow

Do you work away for long stretches, energized by a current of ideas and insights? Or are you exhausted by how every day feels like a bumper car ride of stops and starts? Are you craving a day where you can finally get momentum?

We've come this far with you, our noble knight, your quest, your dragons, and your armor. We can't abandon our goofy metaphor now. Let's figure out how to fill your chalice.

One effective way to boost your energy is to work in what's called a "flow state." This term was coined by psychologist Mihaly Csikszentmihalyi to describe the experience of "effortless attention," intrinsic motivation, and a flood of positive emotions and self-worth. Sounds amazing, doesn't it? Working in flow is like filling your chalice under a rushing waterfall.

So, how do you get there?

Make Way for Flow

First, consider the time of day that best suits deep work for you. As we discussed in "Schedule in Slots," there are times in your day when you're most alert, creative, and productive—we called it Focus and Forge time. That's where you're more likely to find yourself doused by a roaring rush of ideas. Don't expect to find flow in the shady valley of your calendar when you only have the mental capacity for tasks like processing invoices, responding to emails, and taking the compulsory online anti-money-laundering course for the seventh year in a row. Be fiercely protective of the time slots when you have the greatest chance of getting into a flow state.

Make your physical surroundings work as well. That means finding a space with no clutter and nothing that will distract you. If you have an office with a door, close it. If not, where can you find a hiding spot, preferably one with natural light and a comfortable chair? What barriers can you erect to protect your solitude and avoid interruption? Where will you leave your phone? (You answered that with, "in another room" or "turned off in my bag," right? The shocking-not-shocking reality is, if your phone is in your visual field, even if it's turned off, it's still creating a significant distraction that slows your productivity and hampers the quality of your work.) It might even help to have a designated space for this kind of work, so your brain comes to associate the spot with deep work.

Protect your fortress of flow.

Now you've built the perfect fortress of flow, you need to figure out what you're going to create in it.

You're more likely to get into a state of flow if you set a clear and achievable goal for your time. If you aim to write the next great novel, you're probably aiming too high, and frustration will set in. Instead, set a goal that's tough but achievable.

When I need to write an article that I find daunting, I don't set out to write a full draft. The thought of going from a blank screen (with that nasty blinking cursor goading me) to complete paragraphs feels like climbing a steep hill. Instead, I liberate myself by setting a lower goal—I just need to build an outline. Bullet points feel doable. It still requires rigorous thinking to arrive at my unique point of view on a topic, but it doesn't add the extra energy drain of needing fully formed prose. I'm starting on a downhill to gain momentum.

Mise En Place

I've watched enough Food Network shows to know that great chefs are often in a flow state, but I've struggled to recreate that feeling in my own kitchen. The difference is that chefs are strict adherents to the culinary practice of mise en place, or everything in its place. The idea is that you have all the ingredients prepared and waiting before you assemble them. The same holds for your work.

If you're sitting down to write a proposal, you'd work more efficiently if all the ingredients are ready to go. Instead, in a desire to be productive and efficient, it's more likely you dive in and then discover later what you don't have. Then you're bogged down with the high switching costs of opening new applications, toggling between tabs, and even waiting for your colleagues to send you what you need.

We both know that if you have to open your email to retrieve a file, you're breaking the flow and making yourself susceptible to getting derailed. How often have you opened your inbox, Teams, or Slack to get one thing, only to spend 15 minutes responding to messages from other people? Recently, I was working on a proposal and needed a file that the client had emailed to me. I opened the mail app, saw a new message from a different client, responded to that email, and closed the app. I felt a brief rush of pride that I had not been distracted by LinkedIn or the red circle showing I had new text messages. That was until I realized that I hadn't even retrieved the file I'd initially gone in for. Cue full body sigh.

When you want to be fully engrossed in an activity, do the work beforehand so you won't need to interrupt your flow to finish the task. Assemble your mise en place.

Don't Edit While Creating

One of the best lessons I learned for getting into flow and staying there was from Dr. Nick Morgan. He taught me to separate creation from editing. Editing as you go is like continually damming the flow. And worse, shifting into editor mode isn't just slowing you down and diluting your attention, it's putting you into critic mode. Your nasty narrator starts nitpicking, slagging you, raising doubts. (*If I leave that em dash, will everyone think I let AI write this?*) Now you're back in the emotional hijack scenario, which is the opposite of letting it flow. My friend Mike Ganino has a great expression for this, and the T-shirts to match. He says, "Don't backspace yourself."

If you can get out of your own way and let the speed pick up on the downhill, you'll give yourself more raw material to work with. Then, you can use another session to get into the flow of editing. I know this from experience. When I wrote my first solo book, my writing coach Nick Morgan allowed me to write a 60,000-word book mostly in the passive voice (I was a recovering academic, forgive me) because he didn't want to stifle my thinking or distract me from my quest. When I finished the manuscript, he pointed out the issue. While my first thought was that my cup was empty and I would never be able to edit the entire book in three days, I was wrong. I spent a weekend on my laptop on the couch searching for every sentence with a "*to be*" verb (is, are, were, was) and rewriting it. I fixed 416 sentences, but it was easy work because I got into the flow.

I don't want you to think that flow states are just for writing. In our 3COze Inc. strategic planning process, we separate the day for capitalizing on opportunities in the marketplace from the day for identifying activities and investments the organization needs to abandon. We want both of those conversations to be ruthlessly focused so the participants can reach a flow state. Putting the two contrasting questions in one session would drain the energy from both.

Consider where you could make changes to fill your chalice from a waterfall, to find flow.

Summary: Find Flow

- Flow is the mental state when ideas come easily, and you make rapid progress.
- Find flow by protecting chunks of time where you can work uninterrupted on achievable goals.
- Make it easier to slide into flow by preparing the materials you need in advance and starting on a downhill to create momentum.

If talk about flow seems Pollyanna-ish and your waterfall is more like a dried-up creek bed, you might need to step back. Where are your sources of energy that are less plentiful but more reliable?

Tap Into Your Renewable Energy Sources

Are you plugged in to a reliable source of energy? Or do you put your head down and one foot in front of the other? Want something better than stamina and stubbornness to get you through the week?

We talked about the benefits of a flow state, but getting there requires being focused and stress-free before you begin. If you're up to your eyeballs in work, pressure, and anxiety, and feeling like your cup runneth dry rather than runneth over, you need a different approach; one that's less like finding a waterfall and more like tapping into a well.

The approach you'll want to take depends on your personality. I remember learning in lifeguard training that some people who are drowning slip quietly beneath the water while others splash frantically and expend their energy in a vain attempt to stay afloat. Well, the same holds true with overwhelming workloads; different people have their own self-destructive ways of reacting, and unless you can pull yourself out of yours, you're in trouble.

Start by understanding and counteracting your brand of unhelpful thoughts and behaviors that deplete your energy, whether that's because they drain your chalice or poison it.

What Do You Do When You Are Overwhelmed?

When you get overwhelmed, do you whip yourself into a froth, pacing, twitching, and doing random tasks? Lots of people feel a frenetic sort of energy when they're overwhelmed. Unfortunately, being more active does not mean getting more done. Often, it means you're starting a multitude of things and accomplishing nothing. Even if you're doing things, it's unlikely that you're focusing on the most essential things and more likely just reacting to whatever gets in your way.

If this sounds like you, return to "Chase Outcomes, Not Outputs" in part 1. Energize yourself by doing one activity that will help you produce the most crucial output in service of your quest. Inaction is the problem you're facing.

Here's another possibility. When you get overwhelmed, do you turn to processes, rules, and organization? Do you become a "chalice half-empty" person, bemoaning how unfair your workload is or searching for the origins of what feel like random assignments? You might crave predictability and become principled when you're overwhelmed. But, unfortunately, the fact that you *shouldn't* have to deal with the nature or volume of work you're facing doesn't change the fact that you do.

The antidote for this rigid form of overwhelm is to change your language from "what *should* I be doing" to "what *could* I be doing?" Make a plan for the next few days that puts you in control of any risks and boosts your confidence that order will eventually prevail over chaos. The unpredictability and unfairness deplete you.

Or how about this one? When you get overwhelmed, do you reel against the bureaucracy and mundane tasks that prevent you from getting ahead? You might think it's a competition to see who has it worst or just need others to share in the misery. But while you're busy telling everyone how hard done by you are, or, trying to get attention in all manner of inappropriate ways, your list of tasks is growing, and your list of allies is shrinking.

The cure for this social contagion approach to overwhelm is to switch the nature of your competition from "who has the most to do" to "who got the most done." Changing your scorecard will satisfy your competitive spirit with something more constructive. Getting behind or feeling irrelevant is demoralizing for you.

Complaining makes your list of tasks grow and your list of allies shrink.

One more. When you get overwhelmed, do you collapse on the couch feeling like you can't even sit upright? Your chalice isn't half full; it's smashed on the ground. Did you even have a chalice to begin with? If you become sad and pessimistic when there's too much to cope with, you might take overwhelm personally as a sign that you don't have what it takes.

The antidote for this self-inflicted wound is to do one modest task you feel you can manage. Instead of boiling the ocean, just heat one bucket. Being stuck in the present is deflating for you.

While you have your own version of what stress looks like and things you think and do that zap your energy, you might also have a secondary aspect of your personality that you can call on to energize you—this is your well. For example, my brand of overwhelm is the fourth type. I get deflated when I'm overwhelmed. As a result, I will suffer in solitude. But I also know I'm a social person, so I use that to energize me.

You can tap four wells to fill your cup: connection, action, order, and inspiration. Again, these are personal, so consider which one might work for you.

Four Wells to Fill Your Cup

If you're a social type, the best way to fill your cup is to connect with someone and talk things through. The other person won't likely need to say a word, and just their presence, support, and smile will be all you need to feel more connected and confident. If you want to give them a way to help, ask them to jot down a few notes as you're talking to help you separate the priority tasks you need to address and highlight the ones that you can strike from your list. To tap your well, talk it out.

For the active type, get up and get out. Walk. Fast. The movement will help you process the scrambled thoughts in your head. Open a note on your phone and use voice dictation to document everything that comes to mind while you're on the move. When you get back, you'll be better positioned to think about what's most important on the list and what can wait. Turn the prioritized list into a checklist and start crossing things off.

For the orderly type, build a system. Make files on your desktop, draw a giant chart of everything you need to do and stick it on the wall, use Pareto time blocks, and just do something to show your overstuffed to-do list who's boss. Once you have the system, work it. Break everything down, use a timer, and implement a tracking system to make the chunks of work more manageable. Even a daunting workload will be more doable once you've organized it into submission.

Where's your well? Connection, action, order, or inspiration?

For the creative type, make it inspiring. If your idea of inspiration is to make things sleek, pretty, or visually appealing, grab a notebook and some markers and turn your list into a work of art. In contrast, if your notion of inspiring is more about substance than style, connect your tasks to a higher-order concept that you find more strategic, purposeful, or innovative. If you're "redefining the identity of your company," you might be more energized about tackling the workload than if you're "changing the copy and stock images on the website."

Feeling overwhelmed is, well . . . overwhelming! But it doesn't have to be long-lived, and it doesn't have to leave you spent. Know what type of overwhelm you tend to suffer, stop the unconstructive thinking and behavior that's draining your energy, and tap into your natural, renewable energy sources to feel better.

Summary: Tap Into Your Renewable Energy Sources

- When you're overwhelmed, you waste energy on thoughts, feelings, and actions that aren't helpful.
- Know what situations tend to overwhelm you, and take steps to address the root issue.
- Tap into secondary sources of energy (your well) to provide an extra boost to get you unstuck.

Filling your cup is pointless if the cup is cracked. In an average week, what scenarios leave you depleted? You need more than just new sources of energy; how can you address the energy drains?

Reduce Energy Drains

Do you expend your energy on activities that create forward momentum? Or are you constantly sucked into activities that wear you down with nothing to show for it? Would you like to start spending energy on all the right things?

You've probably had days when you feel like you've done everything to fill your chalice, but it's empty before you know it. That's because filling your cup doesn't help much if it's full of cracks. If you want your energy to last until the end of the day, week, and month, you need to figure out what's draining you and plug the leaks. Let's talk about the things that are siphoning your energy and what you can do to stop them.

Start by paying attention to what's depleting you. Your energy drains will depend on your organization, your role, and your colleagues, not to mention everything that's going on at home. And beyond situational variations, we all have a different energy signature, so something that drains me might be exactly what lights you up. I once had a wonderful colleague who loved nothing more than a day spent reorganizing our team's shared drive. I would rather have mowed a football field with safety scissors, but I was more than happy to let her have the "fun" of managing the drives. The only way to know your energy profile is to spend a couple of weeks logging your energy and mood to see how different activities affect you.

I'll get you started with three common concerns: decisions, drama, and destructive narratives.

Three Draining D's

While scientists are still battling about the mechanisms and root causes, it's clear that making too many decisions is taxing. That makes sense in a thoughtload context because decision-making demands our attention and often triggers our emotions, so it's not surprising that it depletes our energy.

Automation, batching, and checklists: The ABCs of energy conservation.

It may seem like a trivial example, but since I switched to wearing a uniform for my keynote speaking, I notice how much less stressed I am. Deciding what to wear and what my outfit will say to the audience about whether I'm credible, cool, and worth listening to has caused me more distress than I care to admit. I was a nerdy adolescent, and it's been an ordeal to force my self-image to reflect how I've evolved. For each keynote, I now have a killer outfit (that complements the color scheme of the slides), and I have one less thing to worry about when packing. I also bought a complete set of power cords, makeup, and toiletries, so I don't have to think about packing them either. (Now, if only I had remembered my wallet when I went to the airport last month.)

Consider the decisions you need to make on a typical day and look for opportunities to automate routine choices, batch similar decisions together, or use checklists that remind you of the steps or the criteria to streamline decision-making.

Another strategy is to pre-commit to decisions when your energy is high and your thoughts are clear. I try to lock in healthy choices when my energy is high so that I don't have to make an unpleasant decision when my energy is waning. For example, if I need to have an awkward conversation with a client, I send the invite when I'm feeling peppy, like when I've just had a great keynote or made a breakthrough with another client. Similarly, I try to book an extra workout session with my trainer at the end of a session when I'm on an adrenaline high and feeling great, rather than thinking I'll make a good call when I'm mired in writing or flaked on the couch. I think of this as loading my decisions into my moments of strength to reduce my likelihood of making bad decisions in my moments of weakness.

A second category of energy drains is everything that falls under the heading of drama. "Drama" might be a somewhat unfair moniker. What I'm referring to is anything that triggers your emotions and derails your plan. That might be anything from a colleague with a very real and legitimate family issue that requires an outpouring of empathy to a petty bit of office gossip that leaves you worrying Patty is out to get you. These days, drama can be as simple as reading the news or social media and getting emotionally hijacked.

Each time you get taken on an emotional ride, you burn energy. In some cases, it's just not worth it. You're better off avoiding the source of drama or relegating it to certain times in your day or week where it's not a threat to your priorities. Ask yourself whether you have any toxic relationships that you can't afford to maintain.

If you can't (or don't want to) eliminate certain drama-filled interactions, find ways to constrain them. Pop by your colleague's desk 10 minutes before you have to be at a meeting, so you have a fixed end time. Alternatively, set the ground rules for what you will and won't talk about. I'm a fan of offering myself up as a sounding board for someone to vent, or as a coach for how they might address a situation, but I'm clear that I won't be party to complaining or gossiping about someone who isn't present. Constraining might also mean limiting the number of times you're willing to hear the same complaints and saying something like, "You've raised this issue three times, and I've shared all I have to offer. Let's talk about something else." It's easy to get sucked into other people's drama, but you need to decide whether it's worth the investment of energy.

While you might be thinking of all the external demands on your energy, like everyone else's drama, it's equally important to consider how your own thought patterns are burning you out—your destructive narratives. Do you have an unreliable narrator whispering unhelpful things in your head? It might come in the form of impostor phenomenon, where you tell yourself you're not good enough to do the job. It could be perfectionism, where *you* might be good enough, but the work never is. Alternatively, you might engage in unhealthy self-talk about conflict avoidance, where you ruminate and stew in

Is their drama a good use of your energy?

resentment because of a fear of advocating for yourself. These are just a sample of the stories you might be telling yourself that are wearing you out and keeping you stuck. I've included some resources in the toolkit at thoughtload.com to help you reduce the drain from these and other destructive narratives.

Continually exerting energy on things that add little value makes it difficult to keep anything in your cup. Seal the cracks, fix the drains, and notice how much easier it is to conserve your energy for the things that matter most.

Summary: Reduce Energy Drains

- To reduce the energy you waste, eliminate as many energy drains as possible.
- Monitor your thoughts, feelings, and activities to identify what is zapping your energy.
- Take action to reduce energy drains, including unnecessary decisions, toxic drama, and negative self-talk.

Restoring your energy requires you to tap into your natural reserves and to fill the cracks that are draining your cup. But sometimes, you are so exhausted you can't muster the mojo to start. That's when you need to try something completely counterintuitive.

Do More Nothing

Do your weeks and months include time to rest and digest what you're learning? Or do you ingest so much information that you're unable to process any of it? Ready to clear your plate?

My final offering in this part on boosting your energy might sound weird, maybe even ridiculous, when you're buckling under a heavy thoughtload. I promise you that this technique has been one of my most reliable methods of energizing myself, and I've been doing it for ten years. Let me tell you the story of how I learned to get more done by doing more nothing.

Back in 2016, I was watching the Netflix documentary series *Cooked* by the celebrated author Michael Pollan. Each of the four episodes focuses on one cooking method: fire, water, earth, and air. In the one about air, Pollan shares that a person given nothing but flour and water to eat and drink would live for a short time and then die from starvation.

Now here's the cool part. If the flour and water were combined and exposed to the air (where they would pick up naturally occurring yeast and microbes), that dough could be baked into bread that would nourish the person indefinitely. The air converts raw ingredients into something truly alive and nourishing. (Shout-out to my best friend Tracey, who immediately highlighted the scurvy risk. Sheesh, remind me not to use metaphors with scientists!)

Listening to Pollan, I wasn't inspired to create my own sourdough starter and take up bread baking (that had to wait for the pandemic). Instead, I had a giant, cymbal-crashing epiphany that our lives are full of flour and water (we're choking on it), but what they lack is any air.

You probably have amazing raw ingredients. I don't know what's in your brain pantry, but I imagine it's stuffed with customer conversations, news articles, conference presentations, and best practice reports from consulting partners. And of course, your inspiration doesn't just come from things that are directly work-related. Maybe you've traveled and seen how your industry works in another part of the world, or you've seen some ingenious gizmo, or had an inspiring conversation with someone from a totally different background. There's always been plenty to work with; there just hasn't been the time to bring it together and let it bubble and rise. Are you subsisting on flour and water?

Where is your air?

Reduce Input

Adding more air into your life may be harder than you think. We are constantly bombarded with input from all our senses. I hesitate to use the word "addicted," but we're at least conditioned to seek stimulation constantly. When was the last time that you spent a full hour with minimal input? No screen, no podcast, no radio on in the background? When I ask this question, most people search their memories and then shrug, "I can't remember a time recently." When I asked my daughter about it, she recoiled in horror and said, "That sounds excruciating!" Given the state of emotional dysregulation we talked about earlier, I guess it's no surprise that being alone with your thoughts is out of fashion.

How could that change for you?

Are you afraid to be alone with your thoughts?

Where could you insert a 1-hour chunk of low-input time into your week? I can share some of mine for inspiration. Yesterday, I walked 40 minutes each way to a doctor's appointment. I left my earbuds out and let my mind wander. Baking is also a great time for me in the same way others enjoy gardening, because there's something your hands can do while your brain is otherwise occupied. (I do caution against baking when your brain gets too fired up because it's easy to use a tablespoon rather than a teaspoon of baking powder, and that is, totally hypothetically, of course, ungood.) Finally, if I want to treat myself, my favorite hour of energizing, low-input time is getting a massage.

These days, I'm much less likely to be baking or getting a massage. Lately, the biggest boon to my intellectual fermentation is time on planes. A few months ago, when I was preparing to write this book, I was in a slump and unable to come up with a framework I was happy with. Craig and I boarded an early morning flight to Austin en route to a client session. I buckled myself in and then put on a meditation app. After about 40 minutes of air, I couldn't contain the thoughts rising in my head. I turned off the meditation, opened my notebook, and wrote out the entire book outline before we landed. It was almost identical to the content of the finished product you're reading right now. All the flour and water were already in my head; I just needed the air.

The key is not to set out to think about anything in particular. Just make space for yourself and be confident that all the necessary ingredients are already in the pantry—they just need the air. You'll reap the rewards of improved health and decreased stress, but the best part is how much more energy you'll have for your work.

You might be thinking, *Oh sure, sounds good for her, but I can't quit my job to go walkabout!* Let me reassure you that I haven't stopped working. Not even close. I'm still attending meetings to secure new work; assisting several CEOs and their teams; delivering keynote speeches; producing blogs, newsletters, and YouTube videos; and always, always writing. It's the time in between tasks that I capitalize on—and you can too.

Sabbaticals for Thinking

I find that it takes two full weeks with a few sessions of low-input time to see the first green shoots of new ideas. So, here's my challenge to you: For the next two weeks, declare yourself on a sabbatical dedicated to thinking. Liberate a minimum of 6 hours each week to expose yourself to air. Count only chunks where you get 45 minutes or more of thinking time. Do something outside and physical while you're thinking, as much as possible.

During those blocks, eliminate all unnatural input. If you're running, don't listen to music; if you're driving, turn off the radio; if you're on a plane, no movie, no newspaper, no *QSWatermelon* (curse Ann Handley for introducing me to that wretched game)! If you need to get up earlier in the morning to make it work, try getting up earlier for two weeks.

You're subsisting on flour and water. Your work, your ideas, and your leadership aren't as good as they could be. Give them a little air and see how energized you become.

I've been encouraging you to use the Thoughtload Planner as a tool to focus your attention and process your emotions. It's just as helpful in boosting energy. Find out how to use the Thoughtload Planner method to restore your depleted energy in the appendix.

Summary: Do More Nothing

- **When your energy is low, fight the urge to cram in more activity and instead, do more nothing.**
- **Give your brain time to consolidate and connect the ideas that are already there into insights.**
- **Take a two-week thinking sabbatical with multiple sessions of no input.**

Every time you find focus, process your emotions, or restore your energy, the benefits will ripple through the other factors of thoughtload. Pay attention to fewer things and encounter less drama. Experience less drama and burn less energy. Burn less energy and have an easier time focusing. And so on.

When you reward responsiveness, you're rewarding distraction.

PART 4

Focus Your Team's Attention

A leader I worked with, let's call her Rebecca, was struggling profoundly with prioritization. She was smart and ambitious, but that made the task of winnowing down activities difficult because she could make a compelling case for why every investment mattered. As a result, her team was stretched across multiple priorities and working nonstop with no results to show for it. Everyone but Rebecca could see that they needed to do fewer things at once: to focus, get traction, work to completion, then move on to the next priority.

For months, this was the crux of our coaching conversations. But each time we made progress by deleting, delaying, or de-scoping an initiative, one of her team members would call me afterward to ask if I was aware that Rebecca had added multiple initiatives since our last session. I would broach the issue with Rebecca and remind her that her job was to help the team make the hard trade-offs and focus on a small set of the most valuable actions; doing one or two things at a time and then moving on to the next would be much more productive than trying to do everything at once. To her credit, she took the message to heart and stopped adding initiatives. Unfortunately, her compulsion to do more led her to start hiding three projects under one initiative heading, like a mom hiding vegetables in the lasagna. To be fair, I don't think she even realized she was doing it.

At some point, the dilution of the team's resources across so many activities meant nothing worked, and the situation reached a breaking point where Rebecca's job was on the line. Only then did she switch into crisis mode and pick one initiative that would save the team. If they could resolve an urgent supply chain issue, they would solve a lot of problems for the company and rehabilitate their image. The supply chain project became the first and only priority. A couple of team members kept the lights on, but everyone else worked tirelessly to implement the project. It became a nonnegotiable. Anything anyone needed to progress became top priority for everyone. I've never seen her team more productive, more ingenious, or more energized. What they accomplished in six weeks would have taken them at least a year in their former diluted and distracted state. Even two years later, when new challenges emerged, someone would often mention the supply chain project as an example of what was possible when they were all aligned on one clear priority. I won't say that Rebecca is cured of her pernicious predilection for piling priorities, but now she knows that it's an issue she needs to continually manage.

Being a manager is a big responsibility, at least if you care about being a good one. For your employees, you are the key connection to the organization and the primary source of intel on what belongs in their thoughtload: what is important, what is legitimately worrisome, and what is worth the effort. If you abdicate that role, your team members' thoughtload will run rampant, as it did in Rebecca's team. However, if you embrace your role in helping your employees direct their attention, process their emotions, and use their energy wisely, you have the opportunity to not only reduce their thoughtload but also increase their productivity and decrease their stress. Said more directly, you have the chance to transform the experience of work for your team. Whaddaya say, worth a shot?

You signal what is important, worrisome, and worth it.

In leading a team, as in sorting your own life, the place to start if you want to tackle thoughtload is with managing attention. It goes beyond the number of initiatives they have to work on. Employees are bombarded with hundreds of emails, invitations to hours of meetings, and to-do lists that include everything from the most impactful tasks, such as overhauling the customer experience journey, to the most mundane ones, like putting everyone else's dirty mugs in the dishwasher. (I learned that there's an initialism for the latter category: NPTs or "non-promotable tasks." You know these activities are taking up too much bandwidth when the peoples of the interwebs create an initialism for them.) Your team members desperately need your help to figure out what to pay attention to and your support to defend their choices about what not to.

Align Around Your Value

Helping your team members know what to pay attention to is one of your most important roles, but I bet your organization isn't making it easy. Is your team being pulled in too many directions?

If your organization is like most, your executive team lists seven priorities simultaneously, with no guidance on which one takes precedence or what to do when they clash with each other. And while the avalanche of priorities is coming at you from above, you're also in the oncoming path of demands from HR, finance, risk, or compliance, who need everything done ASAP.

Your job is to counteract all that organizational entropy by bringing greater focus.

Name the Team's Quest

To start, your team needs the same centering work you did for yourself. You need to bring them in on the quest. What is the unique value your team is meant to deliver for the organization? What's the most important thing you're trying to change? This is not about listing a bunch of activities; this is about remembering what makes your team so important. Are you there to sell more mortgages? Prevent cyber infiltration? Steal market share with a high-fiber snack that tastes delicious (yes, please!). What are the one or two most important outcomes the organization counts on your team to deliver?

Revisit your quest as conditions change. Consider how your unique value to the organization needs to evolve based on shifting trends in the economy, changes within your industry, or responses to your organization's strategy. I've included a guide for how to facilitate this discussion with your team in the toolkit at thoughtload.com.

This conversation will focus your team's attention, and it's equally effective in boosting their energy. Many of us have lost sight of the importance of our roles; rekindling that sense of purpose is powerful.

With the benefit of a compelling quest to work toward, consider what key outputs are required. What does the team need to deliver to create the change you're looking for? What outputs have the highest ROI or likelihood of success?

Once your desired outcome is more obvious, your required outputs might shift considerably. I worked with a team at a municipal utility that was responsible for preparing all the materials for the board of directors. They had been production-focused with no clear sense of effectiveness. When they articulated that their outcome was to ensure the board's confidence in management, they realized they had been missing several key outputs. They didn't just need to deliver a standard, error-free presentation on time; they needed to demonstrate proactivity in identifying and addressing risks, remediation of issues, and scenario and succession planning for the future. (As an aside, in my experience, leaders pay a high price in thoughtload for missing this lens on their relationship with the board. If you don't do the things to earn their confidence, board members will dilute your attention across ridiculous, often trivial issues, trigger anxiety over your worthiness and job security, and defuse the energy of the organization by playing whack-a-mole with requests.)

Finally, ensure each team member knows the activities that have the highest value in service of those outputs.

I'll give you another example. A team I worked with at a property management company identified one of its most important outcomes: no bad tenants. Bad tenants are those who damage rental units, which not only requires expensive repairs but also delays the next renter's move-in date, leaving the company without revenue for a period. With this outcome in mind, each department got creative about outputs that might help. They generated a great list, including improved screening procedures and more detailed instructions on expectations for upkeep. It turned out that they had specific standards for proper upkeep that they used internally but had never shared them with renters. One participant agreed to lead the creation of new tools. That led to a conversation about doing more upfront, proactive activities to set tenants up for success on move-in day, thereby reducing the time and effort required for remediation activities once things had gone wrong. Every person in the room left with a sense of ownership for reducing the number of destructive tenants and a clear path to the outputs and activities they were responsible for delivering to make that happen.

Others' Quests

Once your team members understand the most important outcomes they need to deliver and the outputs and activities that are required to get there, you need to help them think through their contributions to other teams' quests. In most modern, cross-functional organizations, a significant amount of time goes into supporting other departments in delivering their key outputs. In a corporate environment, that might be a communications team supporting a line leader to deliver a town hall program. In a professional services firm, it could be an account team sharing insights with the head of the industry pursuit team. In a not-for-profit organization, it might be the education team getting all hands on deck to support the annual fundraising gala. What are other teams counting on you to deliver? What additional tasks are you expected to complete because you're part of the organization? Linger on these conversations for a while.

How should you prioritize those demands on your team's time, energy, and attention? Which are more worthy? Which are more urgent? What should folks do if the ask will detract from their ability to deliver their own outputs? Which quests will your team support and which will you not?

An engineering team we worked with was asked to reduce its headcount and get ruthlessly focused on shipping new features. Achieving this required clarity around the most important outcome: enhancing the perception of the product among enterprise customers. Next, it required difficult trade-offs about which additional quests they would take on. They realized that two engineers were fully engaged in supporting marketing to manage the website. After some uncomfortable conversations and the realization that the website tasks didn't require specialized knowledge, the engineering team decided that they would stop doing this work and leave it to the marketing team to contract external engineers for it. One fewer quest for them to pursue.

Which quests will your team support and which will you not?

Side Quests

Finally, you need to help your team understand which side quests are worthwhile. What are all the demands on your attention that detract from your producing meaningful outputs and outcomes? Some of these are necessary activities while others are make-work projects. Some are urgent and require your immediate attention, while others can wait until a more convenient time. I cannot emphasize enough how much your team is counting on you to help them understand the difference and to take the necessary organizational steps to manage those who are cajoling, screaming, or nagging them in hopes of siphoning off their attention.

Summary: Align Around Your Value

- Articulate the outcomes your organization is counting on your team to deliver.
- Define the outputs and activities required to deliver the required outcomes.
- Prioritize your team's engagement with other teams and on side quests and help them defend those choices.

Your team likely will be willing to take part in your quest. But at some point, someone will roll their eyes and say, "Yeah, sure, if that's all I had to do, I'd be golden!" A lot is going on that, as a manager, you aren't aware of. You need to find out what.

Expose Unseen Work

You need to support your team members in allocating their time, but do you even know what's on their priority list? Are you aware of everything they are being drawn into?

While it seems as if managers should be involved in the requests that come from other parts of the organization, more often than not, things slip into your team members' calendars or inboxes without you knowing. That makes it hard for you to add value in prioritizing and precludes you from defending them against unreasonable or untimely requests.

While the questions in the previous chapter align the team's attention on the right topics, you'll need to delve a little deeper to help individual members know what to prioritize.

When I speak with managers confounded by their team's lack of productivity, I encourage them to do the Unseen Work exercise. It's an audit of how people spend their time, designed to identify the cognitive, physical, and emotional labor your team members are investing as well as give you insight into where their thoughtload is coming from. I've included the instructions in the toolkit.

When you learn what's on their lists, you'll likely be more enlightened but also more perplexed and frustrated, knowing how many things people are trying to juggle. It's a bit exasperating, but it's necessary if you're going to help them pare back their activities to the most essential.

Prioritize Nonnegotiable Work

There will be two types of activities on your team member's unseen work logs. First, there will be necessary and nonnegotiable things that you'll ask them to keep doing. However, even though you are leaving them on the list, you can help economize their attention in three ways. First, consider whether they can reduce the time and effort required for the task. Can they do a scaled-back version? Can they write new content for 20 percent of the report but repurpose the other 80 percent? Can they inform the other team that they can attend for an hour, but not for the whole day? How might they leverage AI to lighten the lift? You might be able to give a few nudges to get them past the way they've always done it.

Second, you can triage each required task. For example, a task might need to be done, but you don't want it to take up any bandwidth until after the month end. Weighing in on the order you want someone to do work can offer huge relief. It helps them know where to direct their attention, reduces their anxiety, and makes them feel more secure because you've approved moving some things down the queue.

Third, now that you know these necessary activities are part of your team member's workload, you can recognize and reward the effort rather than being oblivious to it. If they spend the last Thursday of every month spreadsheet spelunking to generate a custom report, you can bring them a coffee or save up a funny meme to acknowledge their efforts. (Remember, thoughtload is not just about attention; it's also a function of emotion and energy. The small things you do to acknowledge and appreciate their efforts can lower their thoughtload, even if they still have to do the task.)

Minimize Unnecessary Activity

The second category from their Unseen Work inventory is where you can really roll up your sleeves. What's on the Unseen Work Log that shouldn't be done or shouldn't be done by them? What's not a worthy side quest, but rather a dead end, a trap, or a rabbit hole? You add so much value (and bring so much relief) as you help people think this through.

Delete tasks that aren't adding enough value, are vestiges of a time gone by, or aren't getting sufficient returns. (If you're clear on your most important outcomes and outputs, this will flow relatively easily.) Delay activities that should only be tackled after the things that are at the top of the priority list. Finally, distribute tasks that would be more efficiently or effectively done by someone else.

Acknowledgment and appreciation can lower thoughtload.

When I led a team in a consulting firm, keeping up with the unseen work was a continual challenge. Our team was relatively decentralized, with people working on various projects, including some that fell under my purview and others that did not. I had a conversation with a top-notch team member that revealed the extent of the unseen work problem. She was one of our leading salespeople and also the subject matter expert on leadership development programs. Her main quest was selling and delivering six-figure programs, but she was being pulled into meetings with the firm's executives about their own leadership issues and also called on by other practices to help them design better programming. That, plus she was the den mother, spiritual guide, and emotional support person for most of our young consultants. We spoke frankly about where her extremely valuable attention was best invested, and she made the calls on what to distribute to others or to diminish her workload by limiting her involvement. Then she had my full support in communicating these decisions to others in the firm.

Trap: My team member was more than happy to say no to lower-value requests, but sometimes, when you look behind the curtain and find people doing things they don't need to do, they resist scaling back. You've stumbled upon their fear of missing out (FOMO). Don't let employees dilute their attention because of FOMO. Ask probing questions to understand what motivates them to attend that meeting, be part of that committee, or be cc'd on those emails. You might need to help them break the habit of being involved in things that aren't adding value, as they're creating unnecessary thoughtload and missing opportunities to process their own workload. Help them come to terms with missing out as the cost of being more productive and less stressed. I've included a script on dealing with FOMO in the toolkit at thoughtload.com.

Doing the Unseen Work exercise might seem like a big effort, but it's the kind of investment that pays dividends. Once you've made the first pass over your team's priorities, updating it is easy. Employees are responsible for maintaining up-to-date priority lists and continually bringing non-core activities to your attention so you can triage them together. You might want to do a team refresh once a month or once a quarter. That should be enough to keep the idea of ruthless focus top of mind.

Summary: Expose Unseen Work

- **Expose the unseen work that is drawing your team members' attention.**
- **Coach team members on how to accomplish necessary tasks with less attention and energy.**
- **Triage low-value outputs and delete, delay, or distribute associated activities.**

Once your team has streamlined its activities toward the critical outputs, you'll have the greatest likelihood of creating the outcomes you want. Awesome, except even that to-do list is still too much for one person. You can give them more tools to create focus.

Shrink Teams, Strengthen Communities

If you counted the time it takes for your team members to attend important meetings, respond to relevant emails, and have necessary conversations, it would add up to more hours than are available in a workweek. Are they involved in too many activities?

Consider the impact of increasing cross-functional teams, matrix structures, and communities of interest on your employees' attention. I understand the rush to collaborate and tear down silos, but in the process, we're removing the boundaries that were protecting people from having to worry about everything. If you did the Unseen Work exercise, you probably have a much better sense of the magnitude of this now.

As a result, people are keen to do exercises like building RACI charts to understand who is responsible, accountable, consulted, or informed about a given activity. I'm surprised how often I'm being asked to facilitate these activities. Normally, there's not much racy about a RACI chart, but suddenly they're sexy.

While much can be gained from assigning responsibilities, RACI charts leave me cold for one important reason: a RACI chart has no category for clueless, off the hook, gone fishin'. What if I don't even want to be informed?

Here's a different option. For each of the essential outputs for your team, assign people to one of three categories: core team, community member, or protected party.

Three Categories for Team Members

Core team members are accountable to deliver the output and associated outcomes. They create the plan, engage the necessary people, drive the project, and follow up. Core team members use their precious Focus and Forge time to deliver this output, and everyone on the team knows they're on point. They are carrying the banner for this part of the quest.

Not everyone needs to be leading the way. (In fact, having too many leaders is a great way to stall a quest.) Instead, assign a person as a community member for an output if they aren't driving, but they're expected to be responsive to requests for their input and support. Community members monitor the topics, attend selected meetings, and jump in to contribute their expertise when needed. They build their schedules with time to accommodate requests and check-ins; remember, we called that Connect and Collaborate time. The core people know they can count on them.

The third category is the one we often overlook. We take everyone on our quests, even when these folks are just picking daisies at the back of the caravan. We need to leave some folks behind to keep the home fires burning. Assign a person as protected if you want them to deliberately tune out from a given output. Encourage and support them to impose boundaries to protect their attention. And if members of the core team need the help of a protected person, remind them they need to reach out proactively to get the protected person's attention. They will have to bring them up to speed and help reprioritize, as the person's commitments were based on not being involved in that activity.

RACI charts need an extra category for clueless.

The chair of an industry association committee I'm a part of does a great job of differentiating between core, community, and protected roles. The committee creates the educational and networking activities for the association, including our annual conference, a learning series, and quarterly in-person workshops for executives from member companies. When I signed on, I agreed to lead the learning series, but to keep the workload manageable (it's a volunteer position), the chair suggested I provide only ad hoc input to the workshops and that I be protected from the significant investment of time and energy required in planning the annual conference. I'm not copied on emails about the event, not in the Slack channel, not in the know at all. I show up to the conference each year as naïve as any other member. Thanks to our chair's great management of the committee, I can do this worthwhile side quest with my attention laser-focused on where I can be of the most value.

Smaller Meetings

Consider how often you use your regular direct-report meetings to do work that requires only a subset of the team. That might be convenient for you as the manager, but at what cost to people's energy and attention? I was in a meeting the other day where only half the team members in the room had any knowledge of the agenda item. It was immediately obvious that the topic was irrelevant to them, as they started picking up their phones and opening their laptops. If I had known that in advance, I would have encouraged the organizer to excuse the folks who were not part of the discussion. It was a waste of 30 minutes for those people who could have been adding value elsewhere. Attention is precious, and your team's distraction is one quick indicator that your meeting topic is less deserving of it than something else.

You probably need fewer meetings with all your direct reports than you currently have. In place of standing meetings with all of them, hold focused and fit-for-purpose meetings of the various core teams, centered on outputs and outcomes. If you're clear who's on the core team, who's a peripheral community member, and who should be protected, you can adjust your meeting structure accordingly. Community members might occasionally join those meetings, but for the most part, they should be able to add value asynchronously in shared documents or offline conversations.

Distraction is an indicator that your meeting hasn't earned their attention.

If your team members spend all week hyper-attentive, constantly monitoring, responding to every email, and offering their two cents, they won't be able to focus long enough to complete their core work. So negotiate with your team about who is on which core team, who is in the peripheral community for that output, and who is protected from this phase of the work. Shrink your core teams and strengthen the community around them. It will make a huge difference.

Summary: Shrink Teams, Strengthen Communities

- Resist the urge to take everyone with you on every quest.
- Identify who is in the core team, who is in the peripheral community, and who is protected from each of your projects.
- Delete most standing meetings and replace them with smaller ad hoc meetings of core team members focused on a specific purpose.

Progress! Everyone understands the most important things to achieve and what they can delete, delay, or diminish. They're aligned around who's doing what. They're ready to get to work, and then something else grabs their attention. You need to manage the biggest distractions.

Streamline Communication

Messages come at your team members all the time, from all directions. They're dropping what they're doing and responding to every notification with the same level of urgency. Is your team strong on vigilance but weak on focus?

Every time an employee receives an alert, they need to figure out: What is it? What should I do with it? What do they actually want? When do they really need it? Now multiply that by the 117 emails the average person receives in a day and add one digital notification every 2 minutes. You start to comprehend the debilitating effect on someone who is trying to create focus and flow.

Trap: If you reward people for being responsive, you might contribute to this dynamic. When you reward responsiveness, you inadvertently reward distraction. Only those who monitor their inboxes and notifications respond immediately. The people who allow messages to steal the focus from their core priorities get back to you fastest. Do you want to encourage that? Discuss your expectations for responsiveness explicitly, including clear definitions of what constitutes "too slow" and "too fast" so that your team understands that you don't want them to dilute their focus during heads-down time. Responsiveness needs to be fit for purpose, not always instantaneous.

Three Strategies to Reduce Attention Theft

The first strategy for reducing attention theft of digital communication is to encourage people to close programs they aren't using, activate do-not-disturb mode, and turn off notifications for extended periods when they work. If it makes sense for your team, consider a regular, recurring blackout time, such as 9:00 a.m. to 11:00 a.m. and 1:30 p.m. to 3:30 p.m. daily.

If that doesn't work, find your own way to carve out a meaningful chunk of time during which people shut out the distractions. Set team expectations about when people will check messages and when they can log out of your collaboration tools. Choose your workaround if someone needs to reach a colleague during the blackout time, such as walking to their desk, calling their cell phone, or sending up the Bat Signal.

If people are resistant to setting blackout periods, dig a little deeper into their worries. What concerns do they have about being less accessible for chunks of the day? What problems do they anticipate if others are less accessible to them? What could you put in place to make it work? In my experience, employees often blame their distraction on their manager's expectations, when most managers I know would be thrilled for their team members to be more focused and productive. The employee's own distractibility, boredom, and diminished attention span make them jones for a new notification.

An audience member at a recent keynote objected to my suggestion that they implement blackout periods in his organization. He is the engineer responsible for the client's power generation facilities, and he needs to know if there is an emergency at one of the plants. When I asked (trying to be as open and nonjudgmental as possible) whether an emergency alert that a plant was down would come via email, he admitted that it would not. We agreed that he needed to leave his phone on, but that he could turn off email and Teams notifications for extended periods without risk of missing something mission-critical. Interestingly, I've noticed this trend in many high-stakes roles: We generalize our level of vigilance to the entirety of our to-do list, jumping on the email about the agenda for an upcoming meeting with the same level of urgency as the message that the reactor core is imploding.

The second strategy to streamline communications is to enhance their quality and clarity, making it easier for people to determine what's needed and when, without requiring a detailed understanding of the message. One of my preferred ways to do this is to set a standard subject line structure that everyone on your team uses. I recommend [action] [subject] [due by]. That might look like, "Approve page proofs by end-of-day Thursday." That way, people can triage their inbox without having to click into the body of a message. Senders need to do more of the work to simplify life for receivers. Put in more effort before you hit send.

If you want to focus people's attention on the right things, establish parameters for emails that make them simple to decode. For example, ask that people start the body of their messages with a clear communication of what is required, such as an executive summary of the entire message. Encourage writers to use bold or colored text to highlight any action items for specific people. Then, define what it means if a person is in the to: field versus the cc: field.

The third strategy is to streamline the number of communication channels your team uses and specify the purpose of each. Invest in establishing the proper channels and determining the notification strategy you'll use for each channel. How will you use email versus Slack or Teams? When is it okay to text or DM versus using the more sophisticated collaboration tools? These tools have different advantages and disadvantages, so it's probably helpful to have more than one, but once you have six, managing them all gets incredibly difficult.

Put in more effort before you hit send.

I was working with a national subsidiary of a large international non-governmental organization (NGO). They were struggling because information was coming in through too many different channels. At the national office, coworkers primarily communicated via email, which was integrated into their MS Office suite and seamlessly connected to the tools they used to do their work. However, because the global organization had thousands of field team members working in remote locations, considerable correspondence was happening via WhatsApp, which also drew some of the headquarters' communication onto that channel. Once Teams was layered on top for project work, they were having to keep an eye on too many different spots and wasting energy trying to find things they needed. To make matters worse, when people were overwhelmed by their inboxes and not responding quickly enough, colleagues would send text messages to get their attention, adding a fourth stream of communication. Ugh. However, soon we established new guidelines and agreed on how to direct communication to the appropriate channel, with monitoring expectations tailored to each channel's purpose.

The Power of Asynchronous Tools

One of the most exasperating thoughtload moments for me is when I know I've seen a message I need to respond to, but I can't figure out if it was in email, text, LinkedIn, WhatsApp, Teams, or Slack. I'm forced to use my clients' preferred collaboration tools, and they all have different ones. At this stage, I'm envious of the *Harry Potter* owl network, where your personal bird makes sure any message gets dropped straight in your lap.

Beyond streamlining real-time messaging, how could you capitalize on other asynchronous collaboration tools like Google Docs, Miro, or Notion? If you turn the notifications off, asynchronous methods allow the receiver to pull the communication at a time that suits them, rather than allowing the sender to push the message at a time when it might be disruptive.

Just beware, asynchronous tools protect attention, but they rely on written communication, which often lacks context cues and is prone to negativity bias. If they are used for the wrong things, miscommunication and friction can ensue. Don't put surprises or contentious information into an asynchronous channel—those are worth saving for live conversations. Remember, the choices you make in managing attention will also impact emotions and energy.

Our desks (and desktops) are riddled with technologies that were supposed to make us more efficient and effective, but have made us more frantic, frenzied, and frustrated. It's hard to ask any individual team member to tackle the issue independently. Instead, establish new team standards and reclaim your attention and focus.

Summary: Streamline Communication

- Assign blackout periods when team members won't be actively monitoring communications.
- Establish parameters for which communication channels your team will use and how you'll optimize them for different purposes.
- Use asynchronous tools to allow people to control when an activity gets their attention.

Training your team to optimize how you all use your time in service of your quest will lower thoughtload enough to concentrate on the next problem. How do you help them alleviate their anxiety and deal with the drama? That's where we're headed next.

PART 5

Process Your Team's Emotions

James took the helm as the new CEO of a mid-sized accounting firm. Although he had been in the industry his whole career, he was new to this organization. Having an outsider at the top was a big change for members of the leadership team, who had mostly been with the firm since graduating from college. James was brought in by the board of directors, who hoped his big-firm experience would help the company achieve its growth aspirations, but they underappreciated the magnitude of the change effort required to get the organization onside.

For his part, James recognized that the firm would need new systems and processes but underestimated the anxiety his team members were feeling and what it would take to overcome the inertia it caused. In his first months, his optimistic attitude and vision for the future were no match for the resistance he faced.

We encouraged James to slow things down and open the conversation up, to worry less about making change and more about building connection. The good news was that his team members were smart, high-integrity professionals who were willing to engage; the bad news was that they lacked the emotional literacy to express what they were worried about. James had to slow the roll, shift to a more measured approach focused on understanding where they had been burned in the past. He gradually built a scaffold of trust; first, by creating a connection by spending time together traveling to client sites and sharing meals, then by establishing his credibility, demonstrating his reliability, and ultimately, modeling integrity by being vulnerable and accountable in the most challenging moments. Once he showed them that he took their concerns seriously and factored them into his decision-making, the team members made steady progress in evolving their systems and processes. James learned the slow and painful way that ignoring the emotional dynamics of the team and relying on logic, enthusiasm, and perseverance doesn't work.

Clarifying your team's most valuable contributions and getting their time locked on target will produce a noticeable improvement in their thoughtload (and yours). But it's not enough. Emotions are easily triggered and quick to spread in a team context. When issues become emotional, all focus goes out the window. Your next job is to help team members work through their emotions so they don't devolve into derailing drama. Now, being on top of your own emotional reactions is one thing, but how do you manage the emotional tenor of an entire team? It's a challenge. But there are techniques you can use that will help people process their emotional reactions more quickly and redirect what they feel into something they can do.

Managers, Not Therapists

I have a lot of empathy for what you're going through as a manager. I've shared the ideas you'll read in this part on processing your team's emotions with my best friend. She manages a large team in a pressure-cooker environment. She asked a great question that I expect you'll ask too: "Who's responsible for an employee's emotional dysregulation?"

How do you manage the emotional tenor of an entire team?

Or maybe you will go straight to, *Why am I responsible for their emotional dysregulation? I didn't sign up to be a therapist!*

Either way.

I'll tell you what I told her: The employee is the only person who can be accountable for their emotional state. You aren't their parent, therapist, or emotional support peacock. That said, you *are* in a position to help them learn to regulate their emotions, and if they get better at it, you benefit as much as they do.

You'll notice that none of the approaches I share in the pages to come are anywhere near therapy or counseling; most don't even address people's emotions, feelings, and moods directly. That's for the best. Empathizing with your team members' experiences and strategizing about how to help them process and move to action is important, but you can't own what's going on inside their heads. Sympathizing (where you absorb their emotional state) will be bad for you and the whole team. If they require more support than you can provide, direct them to your Employee Assistance Program or other online or community mental health resources.

Translate, Don't Invalidate

An unspoken expectation, and not one you're trained for, is that you get your team through the emotional rollercoaster. If you downplay emotional issues, you risk exacerbating your problem. Would processing emotions be more efficient than ignoring them?

I've never seen a manager's firm admonition that "it's business, not personal" or "there's no crying in baseball" have the desired effect on productivity. Earlier, I shared the metaphor of the fire-breathing dragon that occasionally interrupts your knightly quest. The same happens for your team members. Sometimes, people encroaching on their treasure awakens their dragon too.

The most likely reason you're dealing with a person who is angry, impatient, or dejected is that they don't feel heard, valued, or in control. Maybe they're reacting to the less-than-stellar performance review you just shared. Or, you're getting an earful about a rocky relationship they have with a teammate.

The emotional outburst is how they're expressing their social pain (remember, social pain is a very real form of pain humans experience when they feel devalued, detached, or ostracized by the group). So, it's ironic that managers often respond by building a wall that further shuts the person out. Each brick in that wall is a fact, a contradiction, or an excuse, some small message that says, "I don't care about you or your treasure." As the manager, you might feel safe behind your wall, but the dragon is still back there, still breathing fire.

The secret is to curtail your natural desire to put another brick in the wall and instead figure out where their treasure is.

Ways You Might Invalidate

Invalidating is signaling that you don't welcome the person's emotional reaction. You might do it directly by saying something like, "Don't get upset," or, alternatively, by changing the subject or contradicting their point of view. More insidious ways you can invalidate someone are to shift your body language away from them or drop your eye contact.

Trap: Kind, well-meaning managers sometimes unintentionally invalidate people by trying to rescue them from distress. Telling someone, "It'll be fine," can be just as invalidating as contradicting them directly. While you might be expressing a vote of confidence that they can handle the situation, they hear, "You're overreacting." Similarly, trying to find the positive in every situation can feel toxically positive: While you might see the silver lining, they need you to realize it's inside a giant cloud. Even if you intend to alleviate the negative emotion, it can feel more like you're invalidating it.

Invalidation will make things worse. Judging, minimizing, or even retaliating against a person's emotions might cause an immediate backlash and an amplified emotional outburst. Anger might escalate into hostility, sadness could transform into despondency, and concern sometimes descends into fear.

Avoid suppressing emotions—it can amplify them into something more harmful.

Another possibility is that ignoring their emotions allows you to move on temporarily, but at the cost of repressed feelings that erupt later, either overtly or more surreptitiously, and often passive-aggressively.

Finally, continually denying, rushing, or diverting their emotional experiences might cause them to question themselves and become dejected, slowly eating away at their self-esteem.

As a manager, you want to avoid suppressing emotions because it can amplify them into something either overtly or covertly more harmful.

Instead of invalidating the person or building a brick wall to protect yourself from their emotions, you need to find the treasure. That's going to take what I call "open drawbridge questions." These big, generic questions encourage people to open up and lead you to the treasure.

I've included several examples of open drawbridge questions for you in the toolkit, but here are a few examples. "How are you thinking about this?" "What's at stake here?" "What do I need to pay more attention to?" You can also use non-question alternatives, "Take me through your thinking," or "Tell me what I need to know."

Ways to Translate

After asking open drawbridge questions, listen carefully. How you react will make the difference between whether the drawbridge lowers another notch or you get tossed into the moat. The key is to validate what you hear, regardless of whether you agree with it or not. When I say "validate," all I mean is to make the person feel that you hear them, acknowledge them, and respect their right to their perspective. Short, simple sentences make the best validation statements.

Short, simple sentences make the best validation statements.

"You feel we don't have enough people to complete this project by that due date."

"You're concerned that this won't meet your customer's needs."

"You believe you earned a higher rating than you received."

It's okay to take a few degrees of heat off their fiery emotional statements. For example, they might have said, "This is a piece of crap. This is not what our customers are used to from us. Are you fu¢k!ng kidding me?" You might respond, "You're concerned this won't meet your customer's needs." Just make sure you convey the core sentiment accurately.

Once you've earned your way into the castle, ask questions to help the person process their emotions (ranging from what they're experiencing to what they can do to make things better). That means going from their initial statements into questions that might help them reframe how they're feeling or better pinpoint the problem.

"What are the most important things your customer was expecting from this release?" or "Where are the gaps?" Validate as you go and see if you can get closer to the treasure. You're trying to figure out what the issue really is about for them.

Once they've vented their emotional reaction and learned that you're listening, now you can help them figure out what they can do. Generally, the best formula is a hypothesis and an experiment.

"It sounds like the big issue is that we don't have the new ChatBot in this release. It's scheduled for the next one. What do you recommend we try to find a path through until the next release?"

Notice that you're clearing space for the person to name the next step rather than specifying it yourself. If you prescribe the action, all you've done is demonstrate that you don't trust the person to solve the problem. Sadly, you can't process the emotion for them; you have to allow them to process it to the point they're able to move forward. Rushing it won't work.

Trap: One other note—while I mentioned earlier that dropping eye contact can be invalidating, it can also be helpful when engaging in an emotional conversation. For many people, maintaining eye contact can intensify an emotional interaction and make it more difficult to self-regulate. Where possible, find a spot that allows you to be close but facing the same way (for example, sitting side by side or walking and talking). If you're like me and socialized to believe that eye contact is a sign of respect, this might feel awkward, but give it a try and see if it lowers the emotional temperature.

Given all that's going on in our world (and in your workplace), it's almost inevitable that your employees will have emotional outbursts from time to time. Trying to stifle these emotions won't work. Instead, your goal is to help the person process the emotions to extract the useful data, find a way to frame the narrative that protects their treasure, and give them the space to choose a plan.

Summary: Translate, Don't Invalidate

- Emotional outbursts are most likely when the person doesn't feel heard, understood, or valued.
- Resist the urge to invalidate or alleviate the person's upset feelings.
- Ask open drawbridge questions to help them understand their treasure and the steps they can take to protect it.

Helping one team member at a time, you can foster trust and promote understanding, coaching them to process their emotions into useful action. But sometimes, one dragon sets fire to the whole castle, and before you know it, you're in the middle of a team-wide emotional conflagration.

Reduce Emotional Contagion

Working through a team member's emotional outburst is manageable. But the tenor of the whole room will shift toward the pole of the negative person. Are one person's feelings spreading to the whole team?

Emotions spread from one person to another quickly, easily, and unconsciously. This makes your entire team vulnerable to the moods of each member. It also makes it essential that you learn how to amplify positive emotional contagion and dampen the negative.

The most important starting point is to invest in your own emotional health and regulation because the more on top of your own emotions you are, the less susceptible you'll be to the emotional state of your team, and the better able you'll be to help them. Think of all the efforts from part 2 on processing your emotions (interrupting your feelings, identifying your treasure, pairing vulnerability with accountability, and giving to get) as an investment in your emotional immunity.

Then, when you're in the moment, interacting with someone expressing negative emotions (either overtly or more subtly), use these strategies to limit the rest of the team's exposure to their emotional state: Acknowledge what you are seeing; get curious and go the intellectual route; pay attention to what's different; and change the story.

Four Strategies to Limit Emotional Contagion

The best first step is to acknowledge what you're seeing. Because emotional contagion happens without anyone realizing it, the faster you can spot the negative emotion, the less likely it will spread. Rather than attributing their behavior to a given emotion, just zero in on what is directly observable. Are their fists clenching, feet tapping, or eyes darting? Is their volume rising, brow furrowing, or face reddening? As you notice the gestures, posture, and body language manifesting from their emotions, choose not to mirror them.

The faster you spot the negative emotion, the less likely it will spread.

Instead, get curious and become intellectual. Curiosity is a powerful antidote to almost any negative emotion, and this is the perfect time to deploy it. If you find the person's behavior *fascinating* and start searching for its origins, you'll be more cognitively engaged but less emotionally involved. (This is the concept of "feeling for" empathy versus the "feeling with" sympathy we talked about earlier.)

Model this curiosity for your team by asking questions like, "Where are you at?" "What's at stake here?" "How is this landing with you?"

You're doing three important things here:

- You're withholding judgment and showing everyone that it's safe to express emotions.
- You're alerting the team that something is going on, so they're less likely to be affected subconsciously.
- You're teaching the team that there's treasure beneath the emotional reaction and how to uncover it.

Then you can pay attention to what's different. The more you identify with an emotional person, the stronger the emotional contagion. But if you highlight the differences in people's situations, the other team members are less likely to identify as strongly with the emotion.

For example, if someone is distressed because their interactions with finance have been infuriating, you might say, "You have to deal with finance directly in a way that the rest of us don't." Notice that this statement acknowledges and empathizes with the person's plight while simultaneously creates a distance between their experience and that of the other team members.

Finally, you can change the story. The person who is wrestling with their emotional reaction needs to work through the same process we talked about in "Translate, Don't Invalidate." You can help them label their feelings, interrogate them, and choose an action to make things better.

Use a series of questions to move them through this sequence. As they start to express their emotion, slow the conversation down by asking my favorite dragon-taming question, "This is important. What do I need to understand?"

Then ask, "How are you thinking about this?" As they expose their thought process, look for opportunities to reframe their story: "What else might finance be trying to accomplish?" or "What if they are trying to protect us rather than condemn us?" Finally, guide them toward an action: "What's the right next step here?" or "How can you get on the same page with them?" Notice that none of these questions sounds like therapy or even use emotional language. The secret is to help them glean all the insight from the emotions and turn those insights into a pragmatic path forward.

Re-Sync the Team

If the team has been exposed to someone in a bad mood or feeling strong negative feelings, don't let your interaction end on that frequency. Remember, empathy is good, but sympathy is dangerous. You don't want people resonating with unpleasant, unproductive emotions.

The good news is that emotional contagion can be positive too (although negative emotions spread more readily than positive ones). Shift the conversation to someone (or something) that will neutralize and reverse the effect. If you've finished processing the first issue, you might introduce an upbeat topic or ask someone more emotionally buoyant to weigh in.

I used a different option after a particularly uncomfortable discussion with a team at an off-site session. Instead of changing the topic or taking a bio break, I decided to reframe the contentious discussion as a major victory. The team had been deliberating plans to reduce headcount and terminate several employees. The tone in the room was somber, and people were being particularly transparent about their concerns about achieving the ambitious plan with fewer resources. No one felt like talking about the art of the possible.

While they saw doom and gloom, I saw a group of individuals finally forging a team and finding their quest. They were being more candid and vulnerable than ever. So, I matched their somber tone to meet them where they were at, but shifted the content of the message. "Wow! That was a really different caliber of conversation. I'm grateful to Tara for being so forthcoming. It feels great to know that we can bring these contentious issues to the table and help each other work through them." I started to smile as I said it and slowly widened my body language so I could reverse the direction of the emotional contagion. I absorbed their negative emotions and then reframed them in a more positive light. It went a long way toward recalibrating the team in a more positive direction.

Preventing, mitigating, and recovering from emotional contagion takes effort.

Preventing, mitigating, and recovering from emotional contagion takes effort and will likely require new skills for you as an individual and a manager. It's worth it. There are few better investments in your team's productivity.

Summary: Reduce Emotional Contagion

- Emotional contagion can spread quickly and requires that you are on top of your own energy and emotions, so you can help your team.
- Spot emotions quickly and model curiosity and empathy to help the person process their experience without spreading it to others.
- Re-sync the team after an emotional conversation by introducing a positive message and tone.

Reducing emotional contagion is an essential skill but it burns a lot of energy, so you don't want to do it often. How do you help your team members work through increasingly challenging situations without being set off?

Make Discomfort Safe

Part of your role is to help your team members challenge the status quo, make painful trade-offs, and take personal accountability. Each of those actions requires them to feel safe in uncomfortable spots. Does your team experience discomfort as fear?

When we talked about the science of emotions, we explored how our brains experience exclusion from a group as both threatening and painful. The fear of being belittled, challenged, or ostracized can keep your team members in an ongoing state of alertness, making emotional reactions more likely and intense. Taking steps to reduce that aversive experience is worthwhile in its own right, but as a manager, it's also critical for optimizing performance. A person who feels unsafe is unlikely to be creative, collaborative, or constructive.

You need to take ownership of your team's psychological safety.

We owe a debt of gratitude to Amy Edmondson, who coined this term to describe the shared belief among team members that it's safe to take interpersonal risks like challenging existing ideas or suggesting new ones, seeking help or feedback, or voicing concerns. Even the thought of doing these socially risky things can be emotionally taxing for an individual who imagines other team members reacting by being offended, distancing themselves, or concluding they're incompetent.

Over decades of research, Edmondson has demonstrated that without a group's tacit acceptance of these risky interpersonal behaviors, an individual won't be willing to put themselves out there. As a result, teams with little psychological safety don't learn, adapt, and grow.

Lately, perhaps in line with our general emotional dysregulation, I find that people are feeling psychologically unsafe and reacting emotionally to situations that, as an outsider, seem relatively innocuous. Recent examples I've encountered include a person who interpreted a colleague's innocent question about their work as a sign that their colleague didn't trust them. Another was an audience member at a keynote who said she bites her tongue when contentious issues arise because she doesn't have the credibility to say anything to her more senior colleagues. And, it's a regular occurrence for a client to tell me that they can't share a concern with their boss because they'd "get fired." It's hard for me to judge whether the person in a keynote audience is wise to be wary. However, in situations where I know the team and the leader well, I'm confident that many concerns are unfounded. But when it comes to psychological safety, perception is reality.

As a manager, your job is to gradually and deliberately increase the amount of discomfort team members can work through without feeling unsafe.

Conflict Obligations

In my book *The Good Fight*, I share an exercise to help team members embrace their conflict obligations and map the tensions they need among them. It's an effective way of making differences of opinion feel safe and important. The idea is to have each team member describe the unique value their role brings (through their expertise and what they pay attention to), the stakeholders who count on them to advocate on their behalf, and the tensions they are obliged to apply to team deliberations. This exercise is a crucial antidote to the misguided messaging that good team members "pull in the same direction" and "don't rock the boat."

When it comes to psychological safety, perception is reality.

When you reframe the discomfort of debates, disagreements, and dissent as a sign that individuals are fulfilling their responsibility to the team rather than as a sign that their relationships are in jeopardy, you see less angst and fewer emotional reactions. You're trying to reorient social pain so that it's associated with not contributing something of value rather than with putting tension on the discussion. I've shared the instructions on how to do so in the toolkit.

Inviting Dissent and Rewarding Difference

Whether you've done the tension mapping exercise or not, you can invite people to do things that feel uncomfortable. Start a conversation by encouraging the team to broach the difficult issues and make it clear that this is the forum for the discussion, rather than in subgroups or in meetings after the meeting. As you work through the agenda, ask for opposing viewpoints.

I like to frame disagreement as helpful, such as, "I need your help to anticipate what resistance we might face. What might people be concerned about in our plan?" Playing the hypothetical game, attributing resistance to other people, is psychologically safer than owning it. Haven't we all created a little psychological safety at some point by attributing our unpopular idea to "a friend"?

Inviting dissent is necessary but not sufficient to change behavior; your team is watching to see how you react. Saying you want disagreement is easy, but how do you behave when they disagree? If you're going to increase the amount of discomfort people can endure without triggering an emotional reaction and a threat response, you need to reward them when they risk being diverging or challenging, or when they give feedback.

Rewarding their risk-taking doesn't just hold if they raise a *super-important-oh-man-I'm-so-glad-you-called-that-out* point. If their point makes you sad, impatient, or angry, reinforcing their choice to voice it is even more important. The gold star is for courage, not necessarily contribution. Sure, you might need to find a quiet time later to teach them if their points were misguided, misplaced, or mistimed, but the first thing you have to worry about is making them feel it was safe. How you respond in the moment will teach them—and every other person around the table—whether they are safe on your team or that their fear is justified. Your job is to shift the basic wiring that says, "different is wrong" to "different is valuable."

In his great book, *Speak-Up Culture*, my friend Stephen Shedletzky says that for people to take the risk of speaking up, it needs to be more than safe; it also needs to be worth it. That means you need to go out of your way to show how you're using their ideas. When someone dissents, even if you don't change your plan in the direction they'd hoped, find a way to demonstrate that their contribution was valuable. "I'm glad you raised that issue. We're still going to proceed, but I've added in a couple of early measures to watch for that so we can change the plan if necessary."

Sometimes, the gold star is for courage, not contribution.

Be deliberate about making your team members' forays into uncomfortable or interpersonally risky behavior feel worth it. Over time, discomfort will not be sufficient to trigger emotions or to set off the alarm bells. When your team culture evolves so that feeling uncomfortable is still safe, everyone's thoughtload will be much lower.

Summary: Make Discomfort Safe

- Map the tensions required from different roles on your team.
- Reframe dissent from "different is wrong" to "different is valuable."
- Demonstrate that taking a risk to disagree is worth it by describing how you benefited from different points of view.

The sense of safety and value you create for your team around disagreement is a tender, fragile thing. How do you protect it by giving feedback that preserves people's self-worth and standing in the group?

Avoid Passing Judgment

Feedback can be a valuable tool. But the vast majority of what people call feedback is unconstructive, unhelpful judgment that shuts people down rather than opening them up. Do you know how to give feedback that minimizes the likelihood of emotional triggers?

Organizations have jumped on the feedback bandwagon, often enabled by technological tools that make delivering kudos or criticisms easy and anonymous. While the quantity of feedback has grown exponentially, its quality remains suspect. So, I can't end this part on helping your team process triggered emotions without touching on one last source of big, messy feelings—the amount of judgment employees endure on a daily, monthly, and annual basis. Going to work can feel more like being a contestant on a Japanese game show where one has to dodge, hurdle, and absorb all manner of obstacles that aim to hit you in the gut and knock you off balance.

Passing judgment is sharing a poorly informed opinion that lacks both objectivity and insight, often triggering the self-protective fight, flight, freeze, or fawn modes in the receiver. As a manager, you need to learn how to avoid being judgmental. Well, that's not quite accurate. Psychologically, you can't avoid being judgmental; it's another preconscious process. But you can stop your judgments from coming out of your mouth (or being written all over your face).

You can't avoid being judgmental, but you can avoid passing judgment.

Avoiding judgment requires recognizing it. Let's start with some positive judgments to ease in. How about "Good job!" Yup, that's judgment—there's no content; it's all opinion. Other examples include, "That was so innovative," "You're such a hard worker," and "You're a huge asset to this team." Nothing. But. Judgment.

Now, I agree that most people won't throw a fit if you pass judgment that they're awesome, but I was just warming you up for the negative versions. "That was so sloppy." "You're not detail-oriented." "You're wrecking the team dynamic." Each of these messages threatens the person's self-esteem, value, and standing in the group. That's going to wake their dragon.

Just because I want you to put the kybosh on judgment doesn't mean that you should treat people like snowflakes who can't handle the truth. It simply means providing them with information and insight, rather than baseless opinions that can trigger an emotional cascade. You can avoid judgment by objectively describing behavior, giving instructions, offering coaching and advice, and structuring consequences well.

Ways to Avoid Judgment

When you think you're giving feedback, you're likely passing judgment. Feedback is information about what the *other person's* behavior makes *you* think or feel. If you give real feedback, you start by describing their behavior objectively, in a way that isn't surprising to them, and then candidly share what was going through your head. In that case, the emotional vulnerability in the feedback is yours, not theirs.

Trap: Most managers think the novel and valuable information in feedback is about the receiver. It's not. The novel and valuable insight in a true piece of feedback is about you. For example: "In your presentation this morning, you had forty-three slides for a 30-minute presentation. I found that by about slide twenty, I was feeling lost and a bit confused." Feedback is a valuable tool for helping people make more informed choices about their behavior. But it is only meant to share *your* truth, not *the* truth.

Ironically, sometimes managers who are frustrated by overly sensitive employees make things worse by being unclear about their expectations. If you want your employees to do something a certain way, don't judge, and don't use feedback; move straight to instructions: "I'd like you to simplify the description. Please reduce the number of slides to no more than twenty with no more than five bullet points per slide."

An even more empowering approach is to provide coaching. In that case, you let the employee specify the outcomes, and you ask questions, direct their attention, and help them reframe as they devise their own approach. Coaching helps team members learn and grow without treading on their emotions or compromising their psychological safety.

"How do you want the audience to feel at the end of your presentation? Where might you be veering away from that objective? What levers do you have to make your current draft more geared toward that outcome?"

Another approach is to offer advice. Advice draws on your past experiences to help them learn more quickly and with fewer missteps: "I've presented to this group before, and I would make sure that you have your most important points in the first three slides because their attention wanders."

Beware, however, that sometimes, giving advice can upset the person you are offering it to because it makes them feel you are not confident that they can figure it out. (Plus, your advice might be outdated or only effective for you, not them.)

You can also consider consequences. These are essential to healthy teams, but you might avoid them for fear of inviting drama. Don't quit the quest for fear of encountering a dragon! You just need to structure your consequences properly. The best consequences are timely, natural, and situational.

"Timely" means that the consequence come soon after the behavior; that's how we learn best. "Natural" means intervening as little as possible and letting the situation play out. This is the opposite of punishing the person with an outcome that's unrelated to the behavior. For example, if an employee fails to prepare adequately for a presentation, a natural consequence is that they have to face challenging questions from the audience.

Trap: Many managers step in to prevent natural consequences (often because the consequence is aversive for them as well). Do you ever rescue the person because you're afraid of what happens to you if you don't? Rescuing people can be more about your comfort than theirs. If you aren't willing to let a ball drop, the team will learn that they don't have to be accountable because you will be. Sure, you need to know the difference between glass balls that will shatter and rubber balls that will bounce, but if you avoid consequences for fear of creating an aversive emotional experience (for you or them), you're sunk.

Are you rescuing them for their comfort or yours?

Finally, and most importantly for avoiding unnecessary emotional reactions, consequences need to be tied to the person's choices, not to their skills or personality; that is, the consequences need to be "situational." If someone hands in poor-quality work and you need a consequence, use a situational rationale like, "I noticed three factual errors in the first two pages," rather than a personal one like, "You're not detail-oriented enough." When you tie consequences to a person's identity rather than a specific choice they made, it's more upsetting and can lead to lower self-esteem.

A Culture of Psychological Safety

You are not the only one in a position to dole out judgment; everyone on your team, colleagues in other departments, and often your customers and clients are asked to weigh in too. Frame your requests for feedback so they steer people toward objective, constructive, useful information rather than sharing opinions with little insight. These skills can be taught, and you're well-positioned to model them in a way that maximizes the insight they produce while minimizing their emotional toll.

Finally, part of your job is to evaluate your employees' performance. The best way to keep evaluations psychologically safe is to have clear, objective outcome goals from the start of the year and ongoing measurement so the person has a sense of how they're doing. The most upsetting evaluations are the ones that are surprising (they didn't know what you wanted), subjective (they don't have clarity or confidence in the measures), or personal (you're evaluating the person rather than their performance).

Feedback, true feedback, where one person is giving another the gift of insight about the impact of their choices, is a powerful tool in forging strong teams. Your first task is to ensure feedback really is feedback rather than judgment. Your second is to remember that even prime, Grade-A feedback is only appropriate for some situations. Instruction, advice, coaching, and consequences need to play a bigger role if you're going to make learning safe and avoid having it trigger an unpleasant, unhealthy, and unproductive emotional reaction.

Summary: Avoid Passing Judgment

- Organizations encourage feedback but many unskilled people provide emotionally triggering judgments instead.
- Turn to effective feedback, instruction, coaching, and advice instead of judgment.
- Use timely, natural, and situational consequences to promote accountability without making the person feel unsafe.

Teaching your team members to process their emotions will help you tame the dragons and lighten your thoughtload. How do you help them carry the weight that you can't remove? How do you maximize the energy they have and the distance they can go? That's our next problem to solve.

The energy will be
there when you
need to fight
the good fight.

PART 6

Restore Your Team's Energy

We were working with the leadership team at a small not-for-profit agency that supports kids with significant illness and their families. They do meaningful, impactful work. But that work comes at a high cost. The operation runs 24/7 every day of the year, and team members often forget that wearing themselves out will do no one any good.

Their leader, Tina, had a challenging job to do. First, she had to focus her team on the most important strategic projects that would increase their capacity to help families in the future. Second, she needed to make space for the quotidian kindnesses that made a huge difference for the current families in their care. Finally, she had to ensure the team never lost sight of their own families, who needed them to arrive home with gas left in the tank.

This meant Tina needed to be thinking about her team's energy at several levels all at once. At the highest level, she invested significant time in aligning the team's efforts on a minuscule number of initiatives that would have an outsize impact on their ability to achieve their mission. But unlike most leaders, she couldn't let that vital work devour all their time. She needed to protect a significant amount of her team's energy so they could be fully present to the families around them. Instead of being a distraction, those moments reconnected the team to why they were there. Finally, Tina had to be a confidant, coach, and sometimes a cop to make sure that team members weren't giving everything they had to the organization and shortchanging time to recharge their batteries and care for their own families. Helping the team become more aware of how they were using their energy was one of Tina's most important roles.

Your organization might be nothing like Tina's, but your role is the same. How do you help your team find the energy to do what needs to be done without burning themselves out? How do you fill their chalices? Let's consider the steps you can take to conserve and then boost your team's energy.

Cancel Most Meetings

If you lead a team, you spend significant effort orchestrating activity, which probably involves some meetings. But the meetings may have gotten out of control: too many, too long, too boring. Are meetings wasting your team's precious hours?

When I ask people why their energy is waning, the first and most emphatic answer is usually, "Because I spend too much time in unproductive, soul-crushing meetings!" Estimates vary depending on what study you read and what level of the organization you're talking about, but many people spend up to half their workdays in scheduled meetings. Some spend much more.

Wanna be a thoughtload hero? Zap some meetings.

Here are some grounds for canceling a meeting: they have no purpose, they're not timely, there's no agenda, or there's no conflict. (Bonus points if you cut or scale back a standing meeting to get the compounding energy benefits week after week.)

Grounds for Canceling a Meeting

Okay, saying that you have meetings on your calendar that serve no purpose is probably a little harsh, but I bet it's not a stretch to say there are a few where the purpose isn't commensurate with the energy investment. There's a hierarchy of meeting purposes. At the top sit co-creation meetings. In these, you're envisioning something in real time, with dynamic back-and-forths, or hashing out various less-than-perfect options to achieve a meaningful outcome. Time rushes by in meetings like that. At the other end of the spectrum are versions of unidirectional information sharing. These meetings are like grown-up story time but without the cute pictures. You can cut most meetings that veer into story time territory.

Of course, you need to convey the information, but if the purpose of the meeting is to inform everyone of something, could you use a shared document instead? Could you record a video for relevant parties? A video gives viewers the option to watch at 1.5× speed (or more) and allows you to forgo the formalities and folderol that often accompany in-person meetings, not to mention the time going back and forth to the meeting, and the cognitive cost of switching gears on either side of it. You could cut the time required for transmitting information by at least 50 percent and the energy required by even more.

Ask yourself, what's meeting-worthy?

Your topic might justify a meeting, but is the timing right? Do you have the information you need at your disposal to support evidence-based deliberations, or are you all assembling to opine on your observations? I am flabbergasted by how much time is wasted trying to understand and deliberate on issues without any evidence other than "In my experience..." and "I heard that..." If you haven't got the evidence you need to make the decisions, postpone the meeting.

Your meeting might not be timely if you can't act on anything that comes out of the meeting because it's too soon (or too late) to make a difference. Sometimes it makes sense to get well out ahead of something, but often those ideation meetings should be among a small group and outside the context of a full team meeting. What's the most important thing to spend your energy on right now?

Is it really meeting-worthy?

If I had a nickel for every time I've heard an administrative assistant say, "I'm pulling teeth to try to get items for the agenda," well, to be fair, I wouldn't be rich, but I could probably buy a Starbucks half-sweet, extra hot chai tea latte (and there's nothing that boosts my energy faster than that). Why are you holding standing meetings if no one has anything they want to confer with the team about? Why are you forcing it? If there's no enthusiasm for the meeting, address the underlying issue; don't drain everyone further by prolonging a pointless meeting. What's a better use of the team's energy?

Now I'm gonna get a little spicy here. My personal rule is "no conflict, no meeting." If the topic doesn't require the team to be in tension with one another, to contrast different perspectives, and to figure out the necessary trade-offs to optimize the decision, then the meeting is canceled. Many people now adhere to the "no agenda, no attenda" mantra, but I'm hoping "no fight, no invite" will raise the bar. If everyone agrees on everything, save your breath, cancel the meeting.

Conserving Your Team's "Meeting Energy"

I know you don't have the power to cancel meetings you don't own, but how can you help your team conserve their energy and protect them from low-value meetings called by other departments or even by your boss?

A professional services team I work with does a great job of protecting their meeting time while fulfilling team members' strong need for detail. At each meeting, the agenda includes a list of topics covered in primer materials, but they are not meant to be discussed in the meeting. Team members review the content before the meeting to ensure they're aligned with what has been proposed. In some cases, a team member will need to clarify or resolve a minor issue with the agenda item owner in advance of the meeting. This saves the whole team from getting into minutiae that are specific to one or two members. Occasionally, the primer materials spark a challenge that deserves to be aired with the entire team. When that's the case, they use a reserved spot on the agenda to debate the issue so that all perspectives are considered before the decision-maker chooses the path. Other teams would trudge through this material, wasting time, and zapping energy that could be used for more critical parts of their quest.

No conflict. No meeting.

Does your organization have large, low-input meetings? What if your team members took turns attending? Perhaps your all-hands or quarterly departmental meetings are a snooze, or your large project team update with seventy-three people is just an in-person reading of the project Gantt chart. In that case, could you send a smaller delegation and agree to represent one another in the meeting, and update each other afterward?

Another possibility is to send substitutes to meetings that aren't the best use of their time and energy. If the meeting is hosted by your manager or a peer in another department, you might need to send a note to endorse the delegate and share your rationale for allowing the invitee to decline. I bet that gesture would earn you considerable respect from the team member you liberated.

If you're going to help your team expend their energy on the most important things, you'll need to be ready to support and defend their choices. In "Expose Unseen Work," we talked about revealing everything your team members spend time on, which should include a running tally of the meetings they're invited to. As you learn what's expected of them, you can coach them in choosing which meetings to attend and strategize about more efficient ways to meet the stakeholders' needs without sitting through a boring meeting.

Summary: Cancel Most Meetings

- **Cancel or delay meetings if they have no purpose, aren't timely, or have no agenda.**
- **Institute the "no conflict, no meeting" rule and move informational topics to asynchronous forums.**
- **Support your team members in liberating their time from low-value meetings.**

Of course, some meetings are necessary. If they stay on the calendar, how do you organize them for much better efficiency? What does it take to lead a great meeting?

Change Your Meeting Structure

A good meeting can be the most valuable investment in your week. Unfortunately, most meetings start with little momentum and slow from there. Are your meetings set up for success?

The brain can stay in the more advanced, so-called "executive functioning" mode for a limited amount of time. After a period (45 to 90 minutes), it switches to low-power mode, and instead of novel, creative, and balanced thinking, you get habitual responses and default answers. Worse, you probably also get disinhibition, impatience, and a lower threshold for being emotionally triggered. You're back in the thoughtload death spiral again.

That's why it's essential to accommodate these fluctuations in energy, especially in your meetings.

We've talked about how our brains work more efficiently and effectively when we batch similar activities. We violate this principle when we cram strategic, operational, social, and administrative material all into the same meeting.

How could you separate agenda items into similar groups and create meetings that are fit for the purpose? If there is essential coordination to do, use a 30-minute huddle. When I led a large team at a consulting firm, I chaired a weekly huddle focused on coordinating our business development activities. My secret was to host the meeting in a room with no chairs. With nowhere to sit, it was miraculous how everyone kept the discussions moving!

Stop cramming strategic, operational, social, and administrative items into the same meeting.

Whereas some topics benefit from a quick cadence, others need the time, space, and oxygen to do them justice. For example, if you're talking about trade-offs on your product roadmap, calibration of talent reviews, or plans for ERP implementation, rushing through a meaty agenda in a minuscule slot can be demoralizing. To energize these conversations, you need time to diverge, debate, and then align.

Remember when we talked about the different calendar real estate—lush, fertile ground for deep work versus the shady valleys where the wild things are? Yeah, so which real estate are your standing meetings on? Difficult deliberations warrant the prime spots, but your operational huddles don't. Individuals differ, so no meeting structure will be optimized for everyone. However, in general, scheduling the arduous conversations in the morning and reserving the easier ones for later in the day is best. One caveat: You can have one or two high-value meetings a week in your prime real estate, but any more than that and you're detracting from people's individual time for deep work.

How would you reschedule your meetings to match the energy to the task?

You can optimize meetings by following a prescribed structure: starting with a ritual, building on momentum, tackling difficult topics, closing those, and resting and resetting. Let's look at how.

Optimizing Your Meeting's Structure

Consider how you start a meeting. Do you welcome everyone and review the agenda? Start with some small talk and a quick roundtable? Or maybe you all rush in, breathless, take your seats (or Zoom squares), and dive in without any orienting activities at all.

An alternative to those low-energy starting points is to start with a ritual to demarcate the transition from one mode to another and summon the energy and focus to do the task well. What ritual could you use to switch modes, tap into motivation that fills your cups, and connect everyone to the value of the work you need to do?

I'll give you a good example. One of my clients, a large utilities provider, starts every meeting with a safety moment. A team member presents data or research to highlight a previously underappreciated safety risk and offers a few recommendations for mitigating it. While the executives in the room are seldom up on hydro poles or handling live wires, the ritual reminds them that their decisions affect people's lives. It makes them sit up a little straighter.

What ritual could you use at the start of meetings or projects to focus attention and tap into the team's energy?

If you start with a ritual to get everyone's energy focused on what matters, the next step should be to build on that momentum by starting on a metaphorical downhill. The best way to get things rolling might be to reconnect with the most important outcome you're trying to create and the associated outputs the meeting is designed to serve.

Getting momentum will be easier if you align around what you're solving and envision possible outcomes rather than by diving straight into contentious trade-offs, detailed data, or specific action plans.

Now you've reached the spot for the difficult or uncomfortable conversations. This is where you can ask your team to anticipate, envision, strategize, and disrupt. You have approximately 45 minutes here, so ensure you're ruthlessly facilitating the conversation to focus on the most critical topics and productive discussion points.

This time is incredibly precious, so don't waste it. Poor facilitation drains energy. Good facilitation requires stopping the person who starts to weigh in for the third time before others have spoken, pausing to start a parking lot for issues that are best addressed later, reinforcing people who bring productive tension, and cutting off those who are in violent agreement or in love with the sound of their own voices. I've included some facilitation strategies for higher-energy meetings in the toolkit.

Once you've climbed for a while, it's time to lock in progress. Forcing your way to the finish line might lead to running on fumes, clouded thinking, and your emotions running high. The returns diminish at that point. It's usually better to stop, confirm what you've learned and what you still need to solve for, and determine when and how you'll return to the deliberations.

Trap: Perhaps the biggest waste of energy I see is teams deliberating on a decision that has no owner. When no one knows who gets to make the decision, you default to consensus, which is highly inefficient. Have you ever labored to come up with a gutless, hollowed-out decision because that was the only way to get everyone onside? Assign who gets to make the call, provide as many evidence-based, disconfirming, insightful perspectives as possible, and then let the decision-owner choose what they're going to do.

Take a rest. Get up. Move. Mingle. Your brain needs a few minutes to recharge.

Whether your next agenda item is another sprint on the same topic or something new, your brain will need a rest. That's especially true if your meeting is digital. Take a rest. Get up. Move. Mingle. Your brain needs a few minutes to recharge, so get the blood flowing, take a quick lap, hydrate, or grab a snack. Contrary to what one of my clients said while blasting through a proposed gap between agenda items last week, breaks are not "for losers."

If you ignore the natural peaks and valleys of your team's energy, you'll end up with tired, grumpy folks making suboptimal decisions. Restructure your meetings with thoughtload in mind by opening with a ritual, picking up momentum with downhill questions, doing focused uphill sprints, locking in progress, then resting. You can repeat that process for 2 or 3 hours and make significant headway.

Summary: Change Your Meeting Structure

- Start meetings with a ritual that encourages everyone to be fully present.
- Gain momentum with high-level alignment before facilitating efficient sprints of debate and deliberation.
- Pause to lock in progress and take breaks before starting another round of sprint.

Even if you structure your meetings well and facilitate them tightly, at some point, they might come screeching to a halt, unable to progress and with you feeling clueless about what's holding the group back. What's going on that you don't know about?

Pay Off Conflict Debt

If issues are festering under the surface, supporting productive conflict becomes nearly impossible. Because of the emotional stakes, issues might remain unresolved, draining everyone's energy. Is conflict debt burning your team out?

"Conflict debt" is a term I coined in my book *The Good Fight*. It describes the state individuals and teams get into when they avoid uncomfortable or contentious topics and instead sit in grievance without resolving underlying issues. I chose the term because it's much like charging purchases you can't afford to a credit card and then paying high interest and penalties when you carry the balance month after month.

Given that most of us experience social pain and want to feel like we fit in with our team, it's not surprising that we get into conflict debt and struggle to get out of it. People hesitate to address issues that might disrupt harmony, threaten their sense of belonging, or erode their self-esteem. And when thoughtload is high to begin with, mustering the energy to take this kind of interpersonal risk can feel too difficult. This is another vicious cycle of thoughtload.

But when you avoid engaging with a specific team member or discussing a sensitive subject, it has a cost: Resentment eats away at you, and the emotional burden of an unaddressed grievance drains your energy. Yet another example of how the bad decisions we make when under high thoughtload is to beget a higher thoughtload.

At best, conflict debt drains your chalice; at worst, it poisons the well your whole team drinks from.

So, what are your opportunities to minimize conflict debt in your team?

Conflict debt (noun): An accumulation of unresolved issues that slows progress, heightens emotions, and wastes energy.

Normalize Conflict

The best way to deal with conflict debt is not to allow your team to get into it in the first place. The healthiest teams anticipate and proactively broach the issues that might become contentious. The secret is to frame your discussions as productive tensions between different roles, priorities, and objectives, rather than conflict between individuals.

For example, it's completely normal for sales and operations to be in tension; one wants lots of sexy new stuff to sell while the other wants to streamline the product list to make production, inventory, and shipping more efficient. Similarly, when the IT security person, who is trying to lock everything down, is in tension with the IT business partner, who is focused on ease of use for the field staff, it's healthy.

When you map out the desired tensions among the roles on your team and establish a process for working through the necessary trade-offs constructively, you'll be more likely to address issues as they emerge and less likely to accumulate conflict debt that wears everyone down.

In fact, the right productive tension can boost people's energy because it taps into their expertise and allows them to advocate for their stakeholders. Fighting the good fight feels gratifying.

Set Ground Rules

Some conflict feels less like the healthy stretch of tension and more like the destructive burn of friction. When colleagues interrupt, contradict, invalidate, or otherwise shut one another down, they trigger the fear of exclusion and social pain. The target is likely to spiral into a self-protective fight, flight, freeze, or fawn reaction, which will drain their energy. Worse, that emotional contagion will likely spread to other team members as well.

To minimize emotional triggers and conserve energy in the room, you must establish clear ground rules for what is and is not acceptable behavior. How will you balance participation and ensure you're benefiting from diverse perspectives? What are your expectations of one another in terms of listening, interrupting, or disagreeing? What are your commitments to one another around getting issues on the table versus allowing them to pile up into conflict debt or go underground into passive-aggressive behavior or warring factions? Developing your conflict ground rules will make it less likely that bad conflict habits trigger emotions and deplete everyone's energy.

One team I worked with struggled with this until we did a ground rules exercise. They coined the term "jousting time" and set out a list of characteristics of how they would behave when they were engaged in a worthy battle. They made laminated jousting time cards that any team member could show when they wanted to invoke the rules. In addition, they had yellow cards for when someone was straying from constructive contribution. I observed a significant decrease in conflict debt when team members used these tools, which made them feel more confident they could work through these issues in a psychologically safe way.

Check Your Balance

Conflict debt can accumulate without you realizing it, so routinely check whether you're carrying a balance. Use your one-on-one conversations to suss out any residual issues or relationship problems team members may be masking and coach them to address these issues rather than letting them fester. Invest some time in a monthly team meeting to solicit any topics that need airing. And ask your team members, peers, and your manager for insight on conflict debt that you might not realize you're contributing to. Don't let conflict debt accumulate without you knowing.

When it comes to energy drains versus boosts, you need to invest to save in paying off a conflict debt. Raising an uncomfortable topic requires preparation, both intellectually and emotionally. However, getting to the other side and finding a resolution for an issue that has been burdening you or the team for a while will feel liberating. Our knight can finally doff the heavy armor worn for protection.

Whatever the source of conflict, broach it with humility, self-awareness, and an eye toward the value of a constructive resolution. If a business decision has been delayed or dragged out, identify the decision-maker, set a timeline, solicit the different perspectives, let the decision-maker choose the path forward, and ask for everyone's commitment to the plan.

If the issue is interpersonal, again, humility, vulnerability, and a genuine desire to understand where the treasure is buried will go a long way. Resist the temptation to build a wall of facts and instead, ask open drawbridge questions (see "Translate, Don't Invalidate"). Use the answers (both yours and theirs) to draw the treasure map, and work together to find a way forward.

I can't do justice to all the ways to reduce conflict debt here. If conflict debt in your team means you're distracted from your quest, getting stuck in the emotional quagmires, and burning energy you can't afford to waste, it's worth picking up *The Good Fight* to help you get your team back on track.

Summary: Pay Off Conflict Debt

- **Conflict debt builds when your team fails to address contentious issues.**
- **Differentiate between constructive conflict (tension) and unhealthy conflict (friction), and set the ground rules for how you will behave.**
- **Identify conflict debts and work through them before they stall your team.**

You'll be surprised by how much more energy your team has when you no longer ignore, repress, or work around difficult issues. Now, one final problem to consider—how well are you modeling the wise use of energy?

Leave Loudly

If you are the Energizer Bunny, relentlessly banging the drum, your team may feel like keeping up with you is impossible, leading them to conclude that they shouldn't bother trying. Does your team need you to be a little less perfect?

One final thing to consider if you want to encourage your team to restore their energy and reduce the burden of their thoughtload: How do you make it comfortable for people to make healthy choices, enforce boundaries, and keep their energy levels up?

How you behave and what that signals can make a huge difference in whether your team feels safe to stop and recharge or whether they work themselves to the point of exhaustion. Do you stop to refill *your* cup?

When my kids were younger, they were both competitive dancers. That meant dance lessons six days a week, often right after school. Fortunately, our best friends' kids also danced, so between us, we had four parents available for driving duty. That was a big help.

Still, for several years, I was on duty on Mondays. To get the dancers to the studio on time, I had to leave my office at 3:00 p.m., about two and a half hours earlier than normal. I needed that time to drive to the school, pick up the kids, take them for a quick bite to eat, and help get eight legs into pink tights and four heads of hair into ballet buns before their 4:30 p.m. class. This could be a reality TV show. (Who am I kidding? It already is!)

At the time, I was a manager leading a team of approximately twenty people. We worked in a big, open space. That meant twenty people noticed the boss leaving at 3:00 p.m. I probably could have slipped away quietly or pretended I had a client meeting, but I decided to do something more important. I started a policy I called "leave loudly." I would wave to everyone and enthusiastically exclaim, "Off to drive the dance bus!"

Everyone knew what that meant. I was going to be offline for a while. I wouldn't be looking at email. If something was urgent, they knew they had to phone, and that they'd be pleading their case on speakerphone with Taylor Swift bops cranked to full volume. They also knew that I'd be back online after 8:30 p.m. when the kids were in bed. They knew all of those things and navigated them beautifully.

The more important thing they knew was that their manager believed life can have different rhythms and that you can contribute fully in ways that work for you and your family.

Now, you might not have to leave at 3 p.m. on Mondays to drive the dance, soccer, or robotics club bus. You might not even have kids or pets that require you to bend your schedule to be home at a specific time. It doesn't matter. You have a life, and you have natural ebbs and flows of energy.

Where are your opportunities to leave loudly in your own way? Send me a note at liane@thoughtload.com and let me know.

When to Leave Loudly

Certain situations call for leaving loudly and are an opportunity for your team to learn by your example.

When the cognitive demands are too high, how might you signal to your team that you're trying to pay attention to too many things and you need to leave the din? Could you announce to everyone that there is too much going on, cancel the standing meeting for one week, and give everyone the slot to work away uninterrupted? What if you took some time in one-on-ones to share the challenges you're facing in juggling too many balls and how the strategies you're using to delete, delay, or diminish activities are taking more of your attention than they should? It can be healthy to admit that staying on top of the endless torrent of tasks is an ongoing challenge. In the process, if you model how you enforce boundaries and deprioritize tasks, it makes your team feel safer in doing the same.

Find your opportunities to leave loudly.

When the emotional burden gets to you, what does it mean to "leave loudly"? No, it doesn't mean storming out of a meeting and slamming the door behind you. That's not the kind of leaving loudly we're looking for. For me, it's announcing that I'm struggling with something or feeling overwhelmed. It's telling folks, I'm going to take a quick walk to work through some stuff I'm stuck on. Some days, it's telling Craig that I'm going for a 30-minute power nap in the middle of the workday because I'm not in the right headspace to be of use to anyone. Recently, I did a version of this with my colleague Matt. I was in a foul mood, and I started off our call by admitting as much. But to pair vulnerability with accountability, I said, "I'm in a foul mood, so I'm glad I'm talking to you right now. Let's start with some fun stuff to get me unstuck." It doesn't happen often, but occasionally being loud about my emotional state speaks volumes about the value I place on self-awareness, emotional regulation, and energy management.

What might work on your team? Is there a code word you could use so the team can communicate that their emotions are running high (or low) and their energy is zapped? Because we've been immersed in this work for a year, my team just talks openly about our thoughtload, how we're feeling, and what we need from each other. It's become a completely normal way to start a conversation or to ask for a reprieve from a request.

When your energy reserves run low, how can you make it clear that you run out of steam sometimes and demonstrate the things you do to tap into renewable sources of energy or reduce the drains? That might mean finishing a big assignment and telling everyone to leave early on a Friday or calling a hiatus in the middle of a meeting if the body language is sagging and folks are looking bored. I don't remember doing exactly that as a manager, but I do remember feeling at my wits' end and calling a break during a particularly stressful project. We all walked out to get ice cream. Other strategies might be to admit when you've been neglecting investments in the things that energize you and commit publicly to getting back to them.

It doesn't much matter what the specific example is; the point is that you're leaving loudly. You're announcing to everyone that it's important to take a break from the thoughtload so you can come back at it with renewed focus, serenity, and energy.

If you don't encourage people to recognize when their energy is low, to halt the things that are depleting them, and tap into their renewable sources of energy, you'll pay in other ways. If you let the chalice run dry, they'll be more likely to get angry, frustrated, or demoralized. They'll spread those feelings to others on your team. And you'll realize nothing meaningful is getting done.

If you want to encourage people to take their thoughtload seriously, try leaving loudly.

Making the Load Feel Lighter

At the beginning of this book, we talked about how thoughtload is an equation with attention and emotions on top and energy on the bottom. We talked about strategies to reduce the cognitive weight and the emotional burden that contributes to the "load" in thoughtload. That said, there's only so far you can go in reducing those things. (As our Austrian tour guide Stephan said when passing a guy spray-painted gold posing as a statue to earn tips, "Job is job.")

As a manager, you need a second approach. You need to focus on the energy your team needs to carry that load. That means connecting them to their purpose, helping them tap into waterfalls and wells of energy, and filling the cracks that drain their energy with little to show for it. When you do that, you'll realize that energy is an endlessly renewable resource and when you invest in good energy management, it makes the load feel a lot lighter.

Summary: Leave Loudly

- What you do to manage your own energy can have a big impact on whether it feels safe for your team members to manage theirs.
- Find ways to "leave loudly" by sharing when your attention is divided, your emotions are triggered, or your energy is flagging.
- Model accountability by specifying what you're going to do to remedy the situation when your energy has fallen low.

Work can't always be more, faster, better. Sometimes your job is to prove that breaks and rest are just as essential to progress as effort is.

A Great Start

Well, here we are at the end. You've come a long way.

For one, you're more aware of the unreasonable cognitive demands you and your team are under, but also more cognizant of the approaches that will help you manage them. You're ready to protect focus and seek flow. Focusing your diluted and distracted attention will allow you and your team to complete tasks faster and feel the satisfaction of making meaningful progress.

But managing thoughtload isn't all about attention. You're more attuned to the emotional burden of daily life and more prepared to engage with emotional reactions, even if it remains uncomfortable to do so. You're ready to empathize with people without inadvertently sympathizing with them. Processing your triggered emotions will allow you to lead your team through sensitive issues without letting them spiral into drama.

Finally, you realize it's not just about the load, it's also about the strength to carry it. You are conscious of people's energy reserves and more aware of how activities wear the team down or build them up. You realize rest isn't an indulgence, and you're ready to use it to restore the physical and mental stamina required to be at your best. Renewing your team's depleted energy will enable them to accomplish impressive things with the benefit of keen minds and calm nerves.

While each of those factors will help you lead your team to perform, produce, and prosper, it's your new understanding of how attention, emotions, and energy each affect the other and contribute to thoughtload that will be the strongest motivator of different choices. You know how shortchanging or taking the expedient route in one area will cost you in the others. Good choices create a virtuous cycle while poor ones trigger the treacherous triad.

> **As you become focused on managing your thoughtload, you'll notice a huge difference.**

As you become ruthlessly, relentlessly focused on managing your thoughtload and that of those around you, you'll notice a huge difference. It truly is the path to accomplish more while enduring less.

Okay, I said this was the end, but that's not true.

It's not really the end because managing thoughtload is an ongoing practice you need to continually commit to. There is no end.

You will finish one quest, but there will be another to take up.

You will coax one dragon to sleep, but it will rise again at a new sign that its precious treasure is under threat. And even if you tame or even slay that dragon, there will be more; yours and those dragons that are alive and well in the minds of others.

And more than anything, you will continually need to find sources from which to fill your chalice and guard against leaks and those who would poison the well.

While you're not at the end, you are at the end of the beginning, and that's a great start.

Acknowledgments

THIS WORK is a product of my interactions with many brilliant, generous, and supportive people, who deserve acknowledgment—and so much more.

To my clients, thank you for your courage, candor, and willingness to be both vulnerable and accountable in service of stronger teams and healthier organizations. Your trust in me means the world.

To the exceptional team at Page Two, you've redefined what a true publishing partnership can be. Jesse Finkelstein, you had me at "Hello." Kendra Ward, your deft editorial touch amplified my ideas without ever altering their essence. Peter Cocking, you wielded your design superpowers to create a book that feels like a life ring, not an anvil. Felicia, Leslie, Carmen, and the whole Page Two crew, you rock!

To those who helped shape the core message, concepts, and early drafts—Karen Wright, John Tigh, Jennifer Krochak, Richa Singh, and many others—this book is better because of your wisdom.

To Matt Jennion, fierce guardian of my thoughtload. I am more productive, sane, and energized because of you.

To the stealth global alliance that is Vivaellipsis—Jenna, Andy, Azh, Lee, Marijo, Donald, Oissim, Nuno, and Tracy, thank you for bringing my work to life in full technicolor.

To Annie Spafford and Kristy Holmes, for helping translate this book into a full toolkit of resources that will help readers put the ideas into practice.

To The Sisterhood—Jessica Holmes, Melissa Leung, Kate Davis, Alyson Schafer, Fotini Iconomopoulos, and Lisa Bragg—thank you for being the safest place to commiserate and conspire (and eat donuts). Thanks for being with me wherever I go.

To my fellow adventurers in the speaking and writing world—Michael Bungay Stanier, Laura Gassner Otting, Ron Tite, Mitch Joel—your example, support, and friendship are a treasure to me.

To Speakers' Spotlight—Martin and Farah, you have created a thriving business and a glorious community. Dwight, Marnie, and the whole team, thank you for your confidence in me and for shining a spotlight on this work.

Thank you to my partners at The Talent Company (Rich and Mel) and The Roundtable Group (Glain, Leah, Colleen, and Ashley). Changing the world one team at a time just isn't fast enough; thank you for extending my reach.

To the incredible, wonderful women who recharge my batteries. My book club: Tracey, Amanda, Susan, Anastasia, and Maxine. And my Keg club: Tammy Heermann, Audra August, and Anna Marie Lavelle. I can't believe we've raised sixteen kids and launched them all. Here's to more time together in the empty nest years!

To my mom: You've listened to every podcast, read every blog, and cared deeply about every big and small thing in my world (or if not, you faked it well). Lucking into you and Dad as my parents was the greatest fortune of my life.

To Kira and Mac, thank you for being the kind of kids who make it easy on a mom. I love that you share your big dreams, amazing adventures, and inspiring ideas with me. I also appreciate that you know when to keep me blissfully ignorant!

And finally, to my husband and business partner, Craig Easdon, for your research and insight that are baked into this book. But most of all, for thirty-two years, being my renewable source of energy and calming force when my thoughtload gets the better of me.

Appendix
The Thoughtload Planner

SEVERAL YEARS AGO, I realized that I needed something more powerful than a to-do list if I was going to cope with my thoughtload. To-do lists are particularly heinous because they keep everything in your attention at once. My to-do lists started out orderly, but over the course of a day or a week, they got out of control. As I scrawled additional tasks, squishing things in or writing up the edge, eventually, my to-do lists were as cluttered as my brain.

Also, I seldom achieved everything on the list in one day, so I was rewriting things on the next day's list, and the next day's... and so on. Each time I had to transcribe a task that should have already been done, I felt defeated and a little delusional to believe that was the day I'd actually get to that thing that I'd been procrastinating for inexplicable but likely profound, might-need-therapy-to-fix reasons.

I needed something better, so I built it, drawing inspiration from Ryder Carroll's bullet journal method. I've been tweaking and iterating the tool for five years to get what I

THE THOUGHTLOAD PLANNER

WEEK OF: ____________

HABIT	M	T	W	T	F	S	S

M ____________
T ____________
W ____________
T ____________
F ____________
S ____________
S ____________

M

T

W

T

F

S/S

NEXT WEEK

IDEAS

need for managing thoughtload. I thought it might be helpful to you, too. You can get your copy at thoughtload.com.

The Thoughtload Planner has three advantages. First, it's analog, not digital. Our brains work differently when we're writing than when we're typing. Added bonus: No notifications jump off the page while you're writing in a paper book!

Second, the planner is as much a practice as a tool. The ritual of starting your day, week, and month by centering on what's most important is part of why it works. Rituals are powerful when you're on a quest.

Third, the planner has room for more than just your tasks. It helps you stay on top of your emotions and energy.

Here's how to use the planner to manage your thoughtload.

Focus Attention

When it comes to focusing your distracted attention, the secret is to create a safe receptacle for each activity until it's time to do it. That is, to keep it out of your thoughtload until it belongs in your workload.

First, pick your ritual planning time. This is a personal choice. I know some people who use the end of the day on Friday to clear their desks from the week that's ending and plan for the following week. I admire those people. On Friday afternoons, I tend to crawl across the finish line. I have a permanent block on Monday mornings for a date with my Thoughtload Planner. You might need to use Sunday evening, which isn't ideal, but if it helps lower your stress to go into the week with a plan, I respect that. As much as possible, pick a time you can stick to because consistency lowers thoughtload.

Use your Thoughtload Planner as your single source of truth on what activities you need to do. Use the slots for each day to note your meetings and appointments. Then slot in your top Category 1, 2, and 3 priorities (see "Make Three Priority Lists, Not One") on the day you expect to do them. Be realistic about the amount of time you have for your quest, other people's quests, and side quests on a given day. Use bullet points that you can cross out when the task is complete. Add new meetings and tasks as the week progresses and cross off the ones you've completed. That's pretty basic, but a big improvement over having everything for the week on one long list.

Consistency lowers thoughtload.

As you plan, look ahead to next week and document any items that need preparation, even if the preparation is just mental. This way, you have a heads-up and time to let the ideas soak in before acting on them. (This strikes the delicate balance between, on the one hand, adding to your thoughtload by dedicating a few brain cells to what's coming and, on the other, giving yourself a heart attack because you ignored the oncoming train until too late.)

Throughout your workday, intrusive thoughts will happen. Some are tasks you need to do. Note them on the day when you can do them. Other intrusive thoughts are things you don't want to forget but don't need to act on. Add them to the ideas box so you don't lose them. I often scribble an idea for a new YouTube video in this box and then go back and collect it when I'm preparing to record a new set.

As you go through your week, cross off things as you complete them. That will lead you to the best spot in the Thoughtload Planner: The little empty star at the bottom of each day. That's what you fill in when each of the things you need to accomplish that day is complete. I love how it feels to fill in that star (go ahead, get a gold pen so it can be your very own gold star). When you glance at your calendar and see the star, your brain immediately knows you can ignore that whole section. What a relief!

Another essential part of managing your thoughtload is reflecting on the week as you plan the next one. Of course, we live in the real world, so you probably don't have all those stars filled in. Which meetings were deferred and need to be rescheduled for the following week? What tasks were you unable to complete? Don't mindlessly copy them to the following week. Instead, consider whether they're still required (still important, urgent, targeted, and essential). If not, leave them behind.

Process Emotions

You can also employ the Planner to help with the emotional side of things. Try implementing one or more of these techniques to anticipate, process, and reflect on your emotions and anxieties.

Once you've populated your Thoughtload Planner with the activities of your week, consider which activities might create an emotional response. Are any of the meetings you have lined up likely to be contentious, or heated, or demoralizing? Being forewarned is helpful.

What's even more helpful is if you can do something in advance to set up the meeting for success. Is there someone you could speak with beforehand to have a quiet, calm conversation that would alleviate some of the pressure leading up to the meeting? If you're expecting to be disappointed by the lack of progress or the quality of someone's work, can you do something to alter that instead of being resigned to it? Your Thoughtload Planner won't just help you manage your tasks; it can help you manage your emotional investment in those tasks.

Reflect on any activities you've been procrastinating as well. Procrastination has emotional underpinnings. For any task that you've written on your priority list multiple times without tackling it, do a little digging. What story are you telling yourself to justify postponing it? Is there something you're worried about or an outcome you're afraid of?

What's the emotional issue beneath your procrastination?

If you need to give an employee feedback that you suspect they won't like, how can you deliver it in a way that makes it more palatable? What might their response be, and what would you do in each scenario? Also, consider how you'd feel if that task were done and behind you. Now, you'll be more likely to do it.

As you review your week, where can you add activities that will clear the air? Some emotional reactions are amplified because your energy is low, and your resilience isn't as high as it could be. Is there a spot to connect with someone at work who lifts your spirits? Is there a 10-minute break where you can get some fresh air, or put on some uplifting music? Make a note in your Planner in the spots where you need to find a micro mood booster.

I've built two empty squares into each day in the Thoughtload Planner for you to use as you'd like. I use one of those to track whether I got my inbox to zero (which is essential to focusing my attention). You might want to use one of those squares to track your mood for the day. Which days felt like a three out of ten? Which were more like an eleven? What was the difference?

Over time, tracking your mood can reveal patterns and provide insights about the activities, habits, and choices that regulate your emotions.

Restore Energy

I have also designed the Planner to keep the chalice full.

There's a section in the Thoughtload Planner for you to document five habits that help you restore your energy. I didn't want to be prescriptive here, so they are left blank for you to fill out. You know yourself best, and you understand the activities that make a significant difference in the amount of energy you have during the week.

I know there are a few good habits that keep me on top of the wave, such as reading a chapter of fiction in the evenings and taking more steps than the default number I get when writing a book (which, incidentally, is about 187).

If sleep is a challenge for you, put that one top of the list. Too little sleep and poor-quality sleep are at the top of the list for depleting your energy. You can either track your sleep quality (there are many tools and apps available these days) or incorporate a behavior you're working on, such as spending an hour without screens before bed.

The fuel you put in your body is another obvious link to your energy. Is there a healthy eating habit you're trying to adopt? If so, add it to the Habit section in your Thoughtload Planner. Right alongside it, you might want to set a hydration goal. Your empty chalice might be less metaphorical than you think.

Whatever you do, don't have all of your energy habits taste like medicine. What are the positive sources of energy you want to remind yourself to soak in? Maybe it's spending an hour a week doing something special with one of your kids, reading fiction, or playing pickleball. Tracking those enjoyable activities, along with your steps or glasses of water, is a good reminder that fun, play, and joy are renewable sources of energy to be prioritized, not indulgences to be sacrificed at the first sign of a busy week.

Each day, take a moment to note how you did on your energizing habits. It feels good to give yourself credit for doing the right things. It's also important to notice if things are getting off track.

Fun, play, and joy are renewable sources of energy, not indulgences.

I mentioned that one of my energizing habits is reading one chapter of fiction each night. Not only is reading fiction a relaxing and welcome respite from screen time, but it has also been shown to increase empathy, which is essential in my line of work. I'm pretty good at always having a book on the go, but occasionally, a week or two will go by without me filling in the reading box once. That's a sign that I'm not enjoying the book. I've learned to stop feeling bad about not finishing and switch to a new story that captivates me. Before

I tracked it, I wouldn't have noticed that I'd been forgoing reading in favor of more time on Netflix.

One final thought: You don't have to track the same energizing activities for a whole year (or even a whole month). Perhaps you've reached the point where one of your habits has become automatic, and it's no longer adding much value to check it off every day. It's okay to drop it from your list in favor of something new you're working on.

The Thoughtload Planner is a one-stop shop for managing your cognitive demands, emotional burdens, and renewable energy sources. For more thoughtload planner resources, visit thoughtload.com.

Notes

The Real Reason We're Overwhelmed

p. 4 *able to return to your task 25 minutes later*: Gloria Mark, Victor M. González, and Justin Harris, "No Task Left Behind? Examining the Nature of Fragmented Work," in *Proceedings of the SIGCHI Conference on Human Factors in Computing Systems* (CHI 2005), 321–30. Portland, OR: ACM, 2005.

p. 5 *inputs between 1,200 and 3,000 times each day:* Rohan Narayana Murty, Sandeep Dadlani, and Rajath B. Das, "How Much Time and Energy Do We Waste Toggling Between Applications?" *Harvard Business Review*, August 29, 2022, https://hbr.org/2022/08/how-much-time-and-energy-do-we-waste-toggling-between-applications.

p. 5 *According to research by Gartner:* Gartner Inc., *Gartner Business Quarterly (Q1 2023)* (Gartner, Inc., 2023).

p. 7 *parenting approach is causing high levels of stress*: U.S. Department of Health and Human Services, Office of the Surgeon General, *Parents Under Pressure: The U.S. Surgeon General's Advisory on the Mental Health & Well-Being of Parents*, August 26, 2024, https://hhs.gov/surgeongeneral/reports-and-publications/parents/index.html.

p. 8 *experience anger or sadness at work on a given day:* "2023 Work in America Survey™: Workplace Health & Well-Being," American Psychological Association, 2023, https://apa.org/pubs/reports/work-in-america/2023-workplace-health-well-being.

p. 8 *such dynamics has declined for four consecutive years*: Six Seconds, *State of the Heart: 2024 Report*, April 24, 2024, https://www.6seconds.org/emotional-intelligence/research/.

p. 8 *is challenging, you also referee conflicts*: The Myers-Briggs Company, "New Research: Time Spent on Workplace Conflict Has Doubled Since 2008," news release, PR Newswire, October 18, 2022, https://prnewswire.com/news-releases/new-research-time-spent-on-workplace-conflict-has-doubled-since-2008-301652771.html.

p. 8 *those people might be easier to handle than the employees who suppress*: Terri Simpkin, "Mixed Feelings: How to Deal With Emotions at Work," Totaljobs, November 29, 2019, https://totaljobs.com/advice/emotions-at-work.

p. 8 *You need to defend against abusive behaviors*: "2023 Work in America Survey.™"

p. 9 *heavy experiences as your employees. Some surveys*: "Future Forum Pulse: Fall 2022—Executives Feel Strain Leading in the New Normal," Future Forum, October 20, 2022, https://futureforum.com/2022/10/20/pulse-fall-2022-executives-feel-strain-leading-in-new-normal/.

p. 10 *our increased arousal reinforces our anxiety*: Lauren K. White, Sarah M. Helfinstein, Bethany C. Reeb-Sutherland, Kathryn A. Degnan, and Nathan A. Fox, "Role of Attention in the Regulation of Fear and Anxiety," *Developmental Neuroscience* 31, no. 4 (2009): 309–17, https://doi.org/10.1159/000216542.

p. 10 *be able to afford a house in the first place*: Julie M. Morgan and Rachel West, "The Hidden Costs of Trump's Economy: Skipped Meals, Rising Debt, and the Impossible Choices Facing American Families," The Century Foundation, November 25, 2019, https://tcf.org/content/report/the-hidden-costs-of-trumps-economy-skipped-meals-rising-debt-and-the-impossible-choices-facing-american-families/.

p. 12 *your motivation may be suffering too:* Six Seconds, *State of the Heart: 2024 Report.*

p. 12 *Passion isn't enough to prevent exhaustion*: "Women @ Work: A Global Outlook—Burnout Survey," Deloitte, 2022, https://deloitte.com/us/en/pages/about-deloitte/articles/burnout-survey.html.

Part 1: Focus Your Distracted Attention

p. 20 *and even temporary depressive symptoms*: Jennifer E. Davis, "Multitasking and How It Affects Your Brain Health," Be Well (Brown University Health), January 26, 2023, https://www.brownhealth.org/be-well/multitasking-and-how-it-affects-your-brain-health.

p. 21 *we get more done, with higher quality, and less stress:* Julia Gifford, "Does the 52–17 Rule Really Hold Up?" DeskTime Blog, https://desktime.com/blog/52-17-updated.

Chase Outcomes, Not Outputs

p. 27 *studies say that's the average*: Trevor Wheelwright, "Cell Phone Usage Stats 2025: Americans Check Their Phones 205 Times a Day," Reviews.org, January 1, 2025, https://reviews.org/mobile/cell-phone-addiction/.

Make Three Priority Lists, Not One

p. 30 *satisfaction, optimism, sense of purpose, and confidence*: Brad Aeon, Aïda Faber, and Alexandra Panaccio, "Does Time Management Work? A Meta-Analysis," *PLoS ONE* 16, no. 1 (2021): e0245066, https://doi.org/10.1371/journal.pone.0245066.

Protect Your Focus

p. 42 *average worker receives a new notification every 2 minutes:* Microsoft WorkLab, "Breaking Down the Infinite Workday," *Work Trend Index Special Report*, June 17, 2025, https://www.microsoft.com/en-us/worklab/work-trend-index/breaking-down-infinite-workday.

Part 2: Process Your Triggered Emotions

p. 48 *chemical, neural, and physiological responses*: Antonio Damasio and Gil B. Carvalho, "The Nature of Feelings: Evolutionary and Neurobiological Origins," *Nature Reviews Neuroscience* 14, no. 2 (2013): 143–52, https://doi.org/10.1038/nrn3403.

p. 50 *social pain similarly to physical pain:* Naomi I. Eisenberger, Matthew D. Lieberman, and Kipling D. Williams, "Does Rejection Hurt? An fMRI Study of Social Exclusion," *Science* 302, no. 5643 (2003): 290–92, https://doi.org/10.1126/science.1089134.

p. 50 *one of my colleagues published research*: C. Nathan Dewall, Geoff MacDonald, Gregory D. Webster, Carrie L. Masten, Roy F. Baumeister, Caitlin Powell, David Combs, David R. Schurtz, Tyler F. Stillman, Dianne M. Tice, and Naomi I. Eisenberger, "Acetaminophen Reduces Social Pain: Behavioral and Neural Evidence," *Psychological Science* 21, no. 7 (2010): 931–37, https://doi.org/10.1177/0956797610374741.

p. 51 *one person's emotional state to another person*: Charlotte Nickerson, "Emotional Contagion," *Simply Psychology*, last modified November 9, 2023, simplypsychology.org/what-is-emotional-contagion.html.

p. 51 *whereas empathy is "feeling for" another person*: John D. Cox, Christiana Mitcheva, and Matthew L. Cole, "The Impact of Emotional Intelligence on Emotional Contagion: Implications for Teams," *Journal of Organizational Psychology* 21, no. 3 (2021): 10–22, https://doi.org/10.33423/jop.v21i3.4306.

p. 52 *the intensity, duration, and expression of their emotions*: American Psychological Association, "Dysregulation," in *APA Dictionary of Psychology*, n.d., https://dictionary.apa.org/dysregulation.

p. 52 *they offer to well-being and overall success*: Stéphane Côté, Anett Gyurak, and Robert W. Levenson, "The Ability to Regulate Emotion Is Associated With Greater Well-Being, Income, and Socioeconomic Status," *Emotion* 10, no. 6 (2014): 923–33, https://doi.org/10.1037/a0021156.

Interrupt Your Feelings

p. 53 *Emotions are data, not directives*: Susan David, "Recognizing Your Emotions as Data, Not Directives," July 20, 2022, https://susandavid.com/newsletter/recognizing-your-emotions-as-data-not-directives/.

p. 55 *most of us think are beyond our control*: Hugo Francisco de Souza, "Mapping Emotions in the Body: Study Reveals Physical Topography of Feeling," *News-Medical*, December 1, 2023, https://news-medical.net/news/20231130/Mapping-emotions-in-the-body-Study-reveals-physical-topography-of-feeling.aspx.

p. 55 *use strategies to regulate that emotion*: Mihaly Csikszentmihalyi, *Flow: The Psychology of Optimal Experience* (Harper Perennial Modern Classics, 2008).

p. 57 *allow them to stay around longer*: Tori Rodriguez, "Negative Emotions Are Key to Well-Being," *Scientific American*, May 1, 2023, https://scientificamerican.com/article/negative-emotions-key-well-being/.

p. 57 *types of troubling thoughts might be beneficial*: Zulkayda Mamat and Michael C. Anderson, "Improving Mental Health by Training the Suppression of Unwanted Thoughts," *Science Advances* 9, no. 38 (2023): eadh5292, https://doi.org/10.1126/sciadv.adh5292.

Know Your Treasure

p. 60 *As Dr. Tasha Eurich's research:* Tasha Eurich, "Working with People Who Aren't Self-Aware," *Harvard Business Review*, October 19, 2018, https://hbr.org/2018/10/working-with-people-who-arent-self-aware.

Give to Get

p. 72 *you'll reframe your own negative feelings*: Bruce P. Doré, Robert R. Morris, Daisy A. Burr, Rosalind W. Picard, and Kevin N. Ochsner, "Helping Others Regulate Emotion Predicts Increased Regulation of One's Own Emotions and Decreased Symptoms of Depression," *Personality and Social Psychology Bulletin* 43, no. 5 (2017): 729–39, https://doi.org/10.1177/0146167217695558.

p. 74 *interacting asynchronously via text messaging*: Doré et al., "Helping Others Regulate Emotion."

Part 3: Restore Your Depleted Energy

p. 79 *to focus, make decisions, and exercise self-control*: Benjamin C. Ampel, Mark Muraven, and Ewan C. McNay, "Mental Work Requires Physical Energy: Self-Control Is Neither Exception nor Exceptional," *Frontiers in Psychology* 9, no. 1005 (2018): https://doi.org/10.3389/fpsyg.2018.01005.

p. 79 *to stem from the buildup of glutamate*: "How Thinking Hard Makes the Brain Tired," *The Economist*, August 11, 2022, https://economist.com/science-and-technology/2022/08/11/how-thinking-hard-makes-the-brain-tired.

p. 82 *that nature includes a view of water*: Matthew P. White, Lewis R. Elliott, Mireia Gascon, Bethany Roberts, and Lora E. Fleming, "Blue Space, Health and Well-Being: A Narrative Overview and Synthesis of Potential Benefits," *Environmental Research* 191, no. 110169 (2020): https://doi.org/10.1016/j.envres.2020.110169.

p. 82 *to manage stress and boost your energy:* Neil Pasricha, "8 Reasons Why It's Time to Become a Birdwatcher," *Neil.blog*, https://www.neil.blog/articles/8-reasons-why-its-time-to-become-a-birdwatcher.

p. 82 *and make you more error-prone:* Abiola Keller, Kristin Litzelman, Lauren E. Wisk, Torsheika Maddox, Erika Rose Cheng, Paul D. Creswell, and Whitney P. Witt, "Does the Perception That Stress Affects Health Matter? The Association with Health and Mortality," *Health Psychology: Official Journal of the Division of Health Psychology, American Psychological Association* 31, no. 5 (2015): 677–84, https://doi.org/10.1037/a0026743.

Find Flow

p. 83 *flood of positive emotions and self-worth*: Mihalyi Csikszentmihalyi, *Flow: The Psychology of Optimal Experience* (Harper Perennial Modern Classics, 1990).

Do More Nothing

p. 101 *and then die from starvation: Cooked*, episode 4, "Air," directed by Alex Gibney, featuring Michael Pollan (Netflix, 2016).

Streamline Communication

p. 129 *add one digital notification every 2 minutes*: Microsoft WorkLab, "Breaking Down the Infinite Workday," *Work Trend Index Special Report*, June 17, 2025, https://microsoft.com/en-us/worklab/work-trend-index/breaking-down-infinite-workday.

Make Discomfort Safe

p. 151 *take ownership of your team's psychological safety*: Amy C. Edmondson, *The Fearless Organization: Creating Psychological Safety in the Workplace for Learning, Innovation, and Growth* (John Wiley & Sons, 2018).

p. 153 *In my book* The Good Fight: Liane Davey, *The Good Fight: Use Productive Conflict to Get Your Team and Organization Back on Track* (Page Two, 2019).

p. 155 *be more than safe; it also needs to be worth it*: Stephen Shedletzky, *Speak-Up Culture: When Leaders Truly Listen, People Step Up* (Page Two, 2023).

Appendix: The Thoughtload Planner

p. 199 *Ryder Carroll's bullet journal method:* Ryder Carroll, *The Bullet Journal Method: Track the Past, Order the Present, Design the Future* (Portfolio, 2018).

PHOTO: SAM WONG

About the Author

FOR THE PAST twenty-five years, Liane Davey has researched and advised teams on how to achieve high performance. In working with hundreds of teams, including dozens of Fortune Global 500 companies, she has developed a unique perspective on the challenges that teams face—and how to solve them. As a keynote speaker, Davey has presented to audiences as big as two thousand and as intimate as twenty. Her clients include Amazon, AstraZeneca, TD Bank, RBC, AMD, Google, Bayer, KPMG, Aviva, and SONY Interactive Entertainment. She is a *New York Times*-bestselling author of *You First: Inspire Your Team to Grow Up, Get Along, and Get Stuff Done* and *The Good Fight: Use Productive Conflict to Get Your Team and Organization Back on Track*. A regular contributor to *Harvard Business Review*, Davey has appeared in several media outlets, including CNN, NPR, *USA Today*, *The Globe and Mail*, and *Forbes*, for her expertise on increasing productivity, enhancing engagement, developing leaders, and addressing conflict. She lives in Toronto, Canada.

Reduce the Thoughtload for Your Team and Your Organization

BY NOW, you're probably ready to reduce not only your thoughtload, but your team's as well. How can you help your team reclaim their focus, process their emotional triggers, and recharge their energy sources? Good news—I'm here to help!

Four Ways to Get Started

Copies for Your Team

Buy copies of *Thoughtload* for your whole team, and I'll send you a PowerPoint presentation and tools to facilitate a discussion with them and start putting these concepts into practice!

Copies for Your Organization

Want to buy books for your entire organization? Contact me about bulk discounts and special offers, including custom editions which can include a foreword from your CEO. (Imagine your whole organization feeling more focused, less burned out, and free to do more great work!)

Speaking for Your Event

Want to be the leader who helps create calm within the chaos? You find the event, and I'll bring the keynote. We'll show 'em why work isn't working—and how we can fix it.

Training Sessions for Employees and Leaders

Need a little more than inspiration to manage the madness? Bring thoughtload training into your organization either virtually or in person. Options range from a 1-hour webinar to full thoughtload training for managers.

Let's Start the Conversation

Send me an email or reach out on social to discuss one or more options for your team and organization. I can't wait to hear from you.

info@3coze.com
@lianedavey
in/lianedavey